NEW YORK
@ NIGHT

A PERSONAL GUIDE TO NEW YORK'S NIGHTLIFE

NEW YORK @ NIGHT

Editor-In-Chief   **C. Dagan McCann**

PRODUCTION DEPARTMENT

Graphic Artist
Bob Callahan

Copy Editor
Cindy Devendorf

Mechanical Production
Regina Vorgang

Copy Editor
Lynn Moore

Artist
Andre Junget

STAFF WRITERS

Corinne Erni	**Lola Ogunnaike**
Craig McGuire	**Gayatri Rangachari**

SPECIAL THANKS TO:

Tad Acker	Peter Colahan	Mark McCann
Fred Afragola	Bob Hamerslough	Jennifer McCann
Steve Avanzino	David Geller	Alex Nephew
Daniel Brewster	Mark Goldsmith	Tom Ryder
Bob Callahan	Alex Kaali-Nagy	Mark Stanich
Deborah Callahan	Karen Kaali-Nagy	John Swanhaus

McCANN/KAALI-NAGY PUBLISHING GROUP INC
Chairman/Co-Publisher   **C. Dagan McCann**
President/Co-Publisher   **Damien A. Kaali-Nagy**

Corporate Address
42 West 73rd Street
Suite 4F
New York, NY 10023
800.830.2002
Internet: http://www.nightlifeny.com

© 1999 McCann/Kaali-Nagy Publishing Group Inc
ISBN- 0-966057-0-5
SAN- 299-688X

Introduction

"All ways led to the saloon. The thousand roads of romance and adventure drew together in the saloon, and thence led out and on over the world."

Jack London, 1913
(Excerpt from John Barleycorn)

A night on the town is more important than you may think. You work too hard to let these brief opportunities pass you by. Each journey into the heart of New York's nightlife should spring from your mind as if it were yesterday, prompting that nostalgic, "You remember when…" Wouldn't it be nice to recall the night you sat wedged between two supermodels at Chaos? Remember the time you pranced on the bar with your bra in hand at Hogs & Heifers? How about that drag queen that came over and belted out a tune for your table at Lucky Cheng's, or that magical night you proposed while overlooking the breathtaking Manhattan nightscape at The Greatest Bar on Earth? That's what it's all about. Isn't it?

Other cities are noted for their nightlife, but New York City always has been, and always will be, the measuring stick. Through our tireless and painstaking research, we looked at the nightlife culture as a whole and selected a choice sampling of 298 establishments that comprise the essence of New York's renowned nightlife. The sights, sounds, flavors and feelings are overwhelming. We've given you something to do every night of the week for the rest of the year, but you're sure to find a second home somewhere. We've given certain well-deserving spots a pat on the head, but we've also knocked a few off their stools.

We now place in your hands this efficient, reader-friendly tool to help you navigate the landscape of New York nightlife. We can only suggest where to go, what to expect and provide tips on what to wear and how much cash to carry. The rest is up to you. So get out there and go for yours.

Reviewing nightlife is almost as difficult as defining it — almost. As strips like Avenue A and Orchard Street enjoy a reemergence, the definition of New York nightlife is constantly changing. We've compiled a clear and concise write-up detailing the elements at play within each establishment, and marked the stand-outs' names in red. For our summation, here's an idea of what we were looking for:

1.) ARCHITECTURE & DECOR

No two spots look the same, but what makes them different? The subtleties of the interior can make or break an establishment. From the interaction of color and texture to the selection and arrangement of furniture and amenities, we looked at how all of these aspects have been maintained.

2.) SERVICE

This involves ascertaining the skill, speed (and attitude) of bartenders, waiters, hostesses, shot girls and other employees. There is no excuse for poor service, especially in a crowded establishment.

3.) SELECTION

What use is an upscale lounge without a wide selection of top-shelf liquors, cordials and cigars? Or an Irish pub without at least six lines of draft? How about a coffee bar with only two types of desserts, or a jukebox still skipping the same CD it did five years ago?

4.) CROWD

Possibly the most important factor on any given night is the clientele. In a city like New York, the varying degrees of styles and attitudes are limitless. However, each establishment has it's own set of norms that make it unique. For better or for worse, these idiosyncrasies were all taken into account.

The sidebar for each establishment is a time efficient way to get the essential facts quickly and clearly. There are six categories plus any additional information listed. This is the breakdown for each category:

Type of Establishment
Bar
Any place that is strictly visited for its 'watering hole' amenities, i.e., pool table, jukebox, live music & libations.

Bar/Restaurant

Not only known as a place to meet, but also a place to eat. Here, the restaurant plays an essential role in the overall vibe.

Lounge

Any bar stuffed with couches (preferably velvet). This being the lounge generation, more and more of these comfort zones are popping up throughout the city.

Live Music

The music is an integral part in the overall make-up of this establishment. Probably the main reason you would be in attendance.

Club

Shake, Shake, Shake…The main theme here is dancing. These are the Studio 54's of the 90s.

Hours

By law, alcohol cannot be served after 4 a.m. in New York, so this sets the stage for closing time. However, some places will be open after that and some will close before. The hours listed are those of the bar and not of the kitchen. Use your judgment depending on the night of the week.

Drink Prices

To arrive at the pricing structure of one to four ($), the following formula has been used: One round of drinks (one domestic bottled beer, one house wine, and two top-shelf cocktails).

$ = $15 and under
$$ = $20 and under
$$$ = $25 and under
$$$$ = $25 and over

Food

Though this is not a restaurant guide, we have included cuisine to aid you in making a call.

Nearest Subway

Although the closest station is not always close, this will at least get you to the neighborhood.

Credit

Most establishments accept all major credit cards (MC, Visa, AmEx, Discover, Diners, etc.) but all prefer the old greenback.

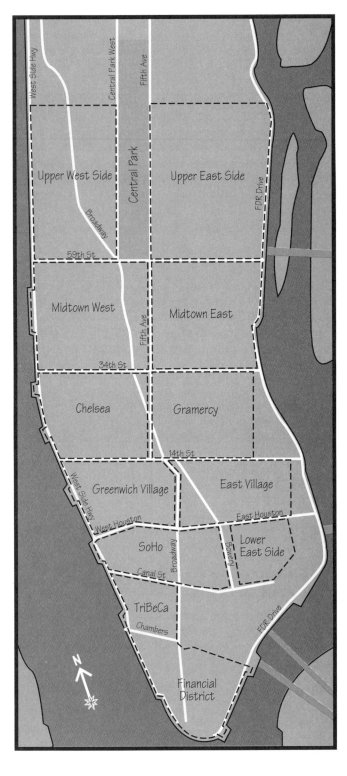

Contents

Upper West Side   9

Upper East Side   17

Midtown West   25

Midtown East   39

Chelsea   49

Gramercy   61

Greenwich Village   71

East Village   87

SoHo   109

Lower East Side   125

TriBeCa (Including Financial District)   135

Index   145

UPPER WEST SIDE

©ANDRÉ JUNGE

*Life on the Upper West Side of Manhattan
pulses with the contemporary sounds
of New York City's artistic, intellectual
and societal elite.*

It's close enough to the city's swirling cultural
epicenter in midtown, yet far enough to shake off
some of the plastic madness and congestion. It's as
worthy of its uptown moniker as the neighbors on
the other side of the park, yet noticeably less
pretentious. From the endless energy spilling out
onto the streets from the rows of popular bars and
restaurants, to the chic sidewalk eateries slightly
hidden away, the Upper West Side is alive.

In the 19th century, the area was a sprawling
suburban landscape considered a peripheral
settlement to the bustling downtown New York City
community. The construction of the Eighth Avenue
line made mass-transit commuting a viable
alternative to crowded life downtown, attracting
thousands to the area. The designation of the
neighborhood as the Upper West Side of Manhattan
soon followed upon the completed construction of
Central Park. The largest contemporary change,
however, came about after construction of the
Lincoln Center complex in the 60s. Its infusion of
artistic and cultural energy planted the seed from
which the neighborhood has grown.

Experience it over a sidewalk brunch at one of the
many neighborhood eateries, or spend a few more
dollars at the area's more famous establishments
like Tavern on the Green or Cafe des Artistes. The
popular nightlife scene in the crowded bars along
Broadway, Columbus and Amsterdam Avenues
echoes the energy and excitement of residents and
visitors alike, so hang on.

1 420 Bar & Lounge
2 Cafe Lalo
3 Citrus Bar & Grill
4 Cleopatra's Needle
5 Exile
6 Hi-Life Bar & Grill
7 Indigo
8 Iridium Jazz Club
   (Empire Hotel)
9 Merchants NY
10 Moonlighting
11 Prohibition
12 Shark Bar
13 Triad (Darkstar Lounge)
14 Venue

420 Bar & Lounge

420 Amsterdam Avenue @ 80th Street
(212) 579-8450

Type of Establishment
Bar/Lounge

Hours
Daily 5pm-4am

Drink Prices
$$

Food
N/A

Nearest Subway
1,9 to 79th Street

Credit Cards
All Major

The secret kept by the black-velvet curtains is that this is one of the Upper West Side's best party places — MTV, CNBC throw theirs here. But you won't know if you walk into this dark, friendly, no-frills venue during the week, and watch locals push tables together or retreat to the elevated lounge area. Come here from Thursday (live band) through Saturday, and follow the neon sign "Downstairs-Bar-Lounge-Pool" to where a determined downtown party crowd dances the night away, plays some pool and continues the party on the couches. Be aware of the dress code — no hats, sneakers or t-shirts.

Cafe Lalo

201 West 83rd Street
Between Amsterdam & Broadway
(212) 496-6031

Type of Establishment
Cafe

Hours
Daily 9am-4am

Drink Prices
$$$

Food
Light menu/ Desserts

Nearest Subway
1,9 to 79th Street

Credit Cards
All Major

Attention to detail is the defining characteristic of this oh-so-Euro cafe. An ever-bustling atmosphere, filled with smart Upper Westsiders, keeps the atmosphere lively all day and all night. Understandably so — with over 100 cakes, pies and tarts, a full bar of top-shelf liquors, wines, aperitifs and cognacs, and possibly the best Sunday brunch on the westside, you really can't go wrong. Add a touch of classical or jazz and you really have a great place to pass the evening and bypass the loud bass lines and smoke-filled rooms.

Citrus Bar & Grill

320 Amsterdam Avenue @ 75th Street
(212) 595-0500

Type of Establishment
Bar/Restaurant

Hours
M-Th 5:30pm-12am
F-Sa 5:30pm-1am
Su 11am-11pm

Drink Prices
$$$

Food
Southwestern

Nearest Subway
1,2,3,9 to 72nd Street

Credit Cards
All Major

You can smell the lemony air and feel the dry desert wind blow through the cactus in this nouveau Southwestern venue. You won't leave thirsty from this 50s-retro diner bar — with over 150 tequila bottles stapled on round chrome shelves. A young, upscale but casual and upbeat Upper West Side crowd enjoys healthy dining to groovy, funky house music in the spacious dining room with enormous floor-to-ceiling glass and wooden doors that open to the sidewalk cafe. Bands and comedians perform at the Squeeze Lounge downstairs (Wednesday–Saturday) where beige retro leather couches, divided by green curtains, invite private partying.

Cleopatra's Needle

2485 BROADWAY
BETWEEN 92ND & 93RD STREET
(212) 769-6969

Named after an Egyptian obelisk behind the
Met, this jazz venue offers a trove of history
and hidden treasures. A mellow 30s uptown
ambiance and great jazz awaits you between
sturdy columns, and the large, square
wooden bar at the center invites you to just
sit there all night and take in the late jam
sessions. The layout is intriguing: a big TV
screen towers above the bar, and the small
stage, where jazz grandeurs play every night,
is sort of hidden in the back. It's obvious
that this is an insider's place — the crowd is
made up of aging jazz musicians, intellectu-
als and locals.

Type of Establishment
Bar/Restaurant

Hours
Daily 3pm-4am

Drink Prices
$$$

Food
Continental

Nearest Subway
1,2,3,9 to
96th Street

Credit Cards
All Major

Exile

117 WEST 70TH STREET
BETWEEN COLUMBUS & BROADWAY
(212) 496-3272

The enigmatic arches and North African
decor at first sight promise an exotic exile
on a quiet Upper West Side street, but the
climate and clientele of this industrial lounge
remain very cool New York indeed. From the
long and narrow marble bar, step down to a
couple of dark lounge areas, divided by mar-
ble pillars with African masks. The upscale,
corporate crowd, sporting intentionally unas-
suming designer clothes, downs Cosmos to
disco tunes. Note: Don't miss the seasonal
garden.

Type of Establishment
Bar

Hours
T-Th 7:30pm-
1am
F-Sa 7:30pm-
4am

Drink Prices
$$$

Food
N/A

Nearest Subway
1,2,3,9 to
72nd Street

Credit Cards
All Major

Hi-Life Bar & Grill

477 AMSTERDAM AVENUE @ 83RD STREET
(212) 787-7199

This lively, black-leather padded Upper West
Side bar and restaurant offers something for
everyone: 70s tunes by Lou Reed or the Talking Heads, posters of 50s pin-up girls, an
Indian elephant god, a big TV screen, a little
sushi bar featuring special half-price days and
an aquarium wrapped in black leather. At 10
p.m. sharp, the panels dividing the bar from
the diner/restaurant are removed, and a DJ
starts spinning his selection of retro music.
The crowd, young and fun-loving, couples,
groups of girlfriends, guys in 70s shirts,
seems to be very at ease with it all.

Type of Establishment
Bar/Restaurant

Hours
Daily 5pm-12am

Drink Prices
$$

Food
Steaks/Sushi

Nearest Subway
1,9 to
79th Street

Credit Cards
All Major

Indigo

487 AMSTERDAM AVENUE
BETWEEN 83RD & 84TH STREET
(212) 362-0373

Type of Establishment
Bar

Hours
Daily 5pm-4am

Drink Prices
$$

Food
N/A

Nearest Subway
1,9 to 79th Street

Credit Cards
All Major

Want to have a blast on the Upper West Side in a pseudo-downtown atmosphere? Come to Indigo and be overwhelmed by a zealot DJ determined to blow your ears off. The bouncy young crowd in this boxy, dark and straight-forward venue with 'bigger than life' surfer paintings, seems to totally love it. They can be found drinking a Surfers on Acid in the front bar while trying to make a connection with someone willing to disappear to the old leather sofas in the even darker back room — above which towers the zealot DJ.

Iridium Jazz Club (Empire Hotel)

48 WEST 63RD STREET
BETWEEN COLUMBUS & BROADWAY
(212) 582-2121

Type of Establishment
Live Music

Hours
M-Th 8:45pm & 10pm
F-Sa 8:45pm, 10pm, 12am

Drink Prices
$$$

Food
New American

Nearest Subway
1,9 to 66th Street

Credit Cards
MC,V,AmEx

$20-25 Cover

From the sensually shaped Merlot Bar with its curving, twisting and bending oversized couches, descend down to the intimate Iridium Jazz Club past a 3-dimensional, iridescent moving picture of jazz veteran Les Paul who performs there every Monday. This intimate 70s underground jazz venue, with intricate crisscrossing ceiling structures and guitar-shaped wall pillows, is visited by a distinguished jazz family of intelligentsia, tourists and passers-by, whose attentiveness seems to be internally felt rather than a polite gesture. Listen to renowned jazz bands such as the Jazz Messengers.

Merchants NY

521 COLUMBUS AVENUE
BETWEEN 85TH & 86TH STREET
(212) 721-3689

Type of Establishment
Bar/Restaurant

Hours
Daily 11am-4am

Drink Prices
$$

Food
American

Nearest Subway
C,B to 86th Street

Credit Cards
All Major

Here is yet another popular Merchants (see Chelsea and Upper East Side) that gets packed with a lively after-work and upscale Upper West Side crowd. The concept works: sensual, soothing colors and shapes, enigmatic but simple Asian artifacts on dark brown-red walls, all adjusted to a hip New Yorker setting. An open, wave-shaped bar is the centerpiece, around which the crowd can observe each other, make eye contact and disappear to a table behind the heavy curtain in the cozy lounge in the back room, or to the large sidewalk cafe.

Moonlighting

511 AMSTERDAM AVENUE
BETWEEN 84TH & 85TH STREET
(212) 799-4643

High and low tech, dark sensuality and understated chic mark this moon-lit Upper West Side secret. Ritchie, who spins an irresistible mix of soul, funk, jungle, Latin and techno records, brings uptown dude, downtown girl, black hipster and white artist in 70s garb together. They dance against gold-framed mirrors and huge bronze panels, or on an elevated dance floor in the back (especially the girls, who seem to have discovered this as their favorite Upper West Side hide). Some cool off on the leather couches, and others, in tight twosomes, dance to traditional Latin rhythms in the intimate downstairs lounge.

Type of Establishment
Bar/Lounge

Hours
W-M 7pm-4am

Drink Prices
$$

Food
N/A

Nearest Subway
1,9 to 86th Street

Credit Cards
All Major

Prohibition

503 COLUMBUS AVENUE
BETWEEN 84TH & 85TH STREET
(212) 579-3100

Americans finally seem to have developed a taste for the forbidden and the immoral. Caricatures of decadent drinking, an elevated back bar with upside-down bottles serving as lighting devices, and a smoky pool table, evoke the ambiance of a 20s speakeasy. But the spacious, stylish locale and the loud crowd, a mix of young professionals and locals, is definitely 90s. They enjoy sitting together at long tables, hanging around the large bar (or the street cafe) and listening to live blues and jazz music.

Type of Establishment
Bar

Hours
Daily 5:30pm-4am

Drink Prices
$$$

Food
Appetizers

Nearest Subway
C,B to 86th Street

Credit Cards
All Major

Shark Bar

307 AMSTERDAM AVENUE
BETWEEN 74TH & 75TH STREET
(212) 874-8500

Queen Latifah, Mase, Jennifer Lopez, and many other hip-hop and rap stars, actors, basketball and football celebrities dine here unassumingly on succulent soul food. Spread out on different levels and painted in beige, blue and yellow, this place is as inviting as a friend's house. You may also come by yourself and hang out at the bar — it's cramped with an upscale, interesting-looking, artsy, professional and lively crowd where everyone seems to have something interesting to say to his or her neighbor.

Type of Establishment
Bar/Restaurant

Hours
Su-Th 5pm-12am
F-Sa 5pm-1:30am

Drink Prices
$$$

Food
Soul

Nearest Subway
1,2,3,9 to 72nd Street

Credit Cards
All Major

Triad (Darkstar Lounge)
158 WEST 72ND STREET
BETWEEN COLUMBUS & BROADWAY
(212) 362-2590

Type of Establishment
Bar/Restaurant

Hours
Daily 5pm-1am

Drink Prices
$$

Food
American

Nearest Subway
1,2,3,9 to 72nd Street

Credit Cards
MC,V,AmEx

Everyone seems to know each other and the common secret of this intimate music and comedy club: this is the place to hear the grand old, and the brand new, seven nights a week. During Sunday night's Soul Gathering, Broadway singers, songwriters and R&B musicians, who haven't signed a label yet, perform for an enthusiastic and interactive audience. Start at the cozy, dark wooden bar and lounge where local artists engage in deep conversations, then venture a few steps down, get a table and enjoy the show on the theatrical stage made of blue wood, mirrors and curtains.

Venue
505 COLUMBUS AVENUE
BETWEEN 84TH & 85TH STREET
(212) 579-9463

Type of Establishment
Bar/Lounge

Hours
Daily 7pm-4am

Drink Prices
$$$

Food
N/A

Nearest Subway
B,C to 86th Street

Credit Cards
MC,V,AmEx

Take your pick at this funky, dark and sensually throbbing cave of cosmopolitan pleasures: stop at the luscious couches, step up to the large bar with an active people-watching scene, where a fashionable, hip, young crowd is chatting away and where guys in suits are on the lookout for female companions to take to the back lounge. Here, elevated mattresses and pillows in metallic, dark stretch-velvet are lit by red lights and watched by a diligent guard! Or venture downstairs into the small disco with carpets and moving psychedelic pictures. A DJ spins a great mix of house, funk, and James Brown.

UPPER EAST SIDE

©ANDRE JUNGET '06

Cradling the nest of wealth and power, the Upper East Side's affluent essence radiates from every crack along Park, Madison and Fifth Avenues — engulfing visitors and residents alike.

From the opulence of the palatial Fifth Avenue highrises facing Central Park to the grandeur of the world-renowned galleries, museums and boutiques that line its streets, the heart of contemporary New York City's high society is firmly entrenched here on the Upper East Side. Some envious of its exclusive and intimidating posterior regard the Upper East Side as absurdly pretentious and dismiss its residents as snobs. The truth is that the Upper East Side is all that, but so much more.

Experiencing the Upper East Side is an afternoon stroll along the famed Museum Mile visiting the Guggenheim or the Met, or treating yourself to a shopping excursion at the ultra-ritzy boutiques along Madison. When night comes down the area shines just as brightly. Unforgettable nights sipping the finest cognacs and delicacies from the area's fine restaurants and supper clubs perfectly accentuate a visit to an art gallery or Broadway show. Loosen your tie and walk a few blocks east to barhop along 2nd and 3rd Avenues, where happy-hours abound as do the throngs of young professionals. For now, sit back, relax, and take it all in.

1 American Trash
2 Auction House
3 Big Sur
4 Brother Jimmy's
5 Cafe Carlyle
6 Club Macanudo
7 DT-UT
8 Hi-Life Restaurant & Lounge
9 Lexington Bar and Books
10 Manny's Car Wash
11 Martell's
12 Merchants NY
13 Tar Bar
14 Trilogy Bar & Grill

American Trash

1471 1st Avenue
Between 76th & 77th Street
(212) 988-9008

Heavy metal blasting, a stuffed buffalo, surfboards on the ceiling, a pinball machine on the wall, a race car, two turtledoves and a partridge in a pear tree. Is it American Trash or all the trash in America? Trash is a neat freak's worst nightmare, but for the record, this biker bar is not dirty, it's junky, on purpose. Judging from the throngs of people that have consistently filled the bar for 10 years (Upper East preps mingle with trailer park chic), American Trash won't be cleaning up its act any time soon. Why mess up a good thing?

Type of Establishment
Bar

Hours
Daily 12pm-4am

Drink Prices
$

Food
N/A

Nearest Subway
6 to 77th Street

Credit Cards
All Major

Auction House

300 East 89th Street
Between 1st & 2nd Avenue
(212) 427-4458

Going once … going twice … sold to the person looking for an occult edge to their evening. This rococo two-room bar brims with Victorian-style sofas made for a king. But behind the ornate gold mirrors and beneath the intense artwork (namely the one of a woman with an indifferent expression on her face, a bloodless lance in one hand, and a severed head in the other) is an air of spookiness. You'd almost half expect Anne Bolyn, (post beheading) to ask what you're having to drink.

Type of Establishment
Bar

Hours
Daily 8pm-4am

Drink Prices
$$$

Food
N/A

Nearest Subway
4,5,6 to 86th Street

Credit Cards
All Major

Big Sur

1406 3rd Avenue @ 80th Street
(212) 472-5009

A popular New York magazine rated Big Sur one of the best pickup places in the Big Apple. There are a lot of hotties, but unlike the actual Big Sur in California there are no sharks here. The scamming is subtle. None of those 'I know you're tired cause you've been running through my mind', or 'Do you work-out? You're sooo muscular' type scenarios. Just conversation as open and clean as Big Sur's contemporary decor. The affordable menu is American continental with a hint of French, but this attractive 20's-early 30's crowd likes martinis more than meatloaf.

Type of Establishment
Bar/Restaurant

Hours
Daily 5pm-4am

Drink Prices
$$$

Food
American/ French

Nearest Subway
6 to 77th Street

Credit Cards
MC,V,AmEx

Brother Jimmy's
1461 1ST AVENUE @ 76TH STREET
(212) 288-0999

In this 'frat house meets shotgun shack' setting, transplanted good ol' boys and their lil' ladies mix it up with the Yankees at Brother Jimmy's. If it's true that BBQ and booze is the stuff that makes America strong, this bar/restaurant — with its lethal concoctions served in fish bowls and its spicy gargantuan ribs so soft they slide off the bone — is doing more than its fair share to make sure the U.S. stays a superpower. Simply put, BJ's rewards customers with a finger-licking good time and down-home Southern hospitality.

Type of Establishment
Bar/Restaurant

Hours
Su-Th 5pm-2am
F-Sa 5pm-4am

Drink Prices
$$

Food
Southern BBQ

Nearest Subway
6 to 77th Street

Credit Cards
MC,V,AmEx

Cafe Carlyle (Carlyle Hotel)
95 EAST 76TH STREET @ MADISON
(212) 570-7189

You think he's a brilliant filmmaker and an even better comedian? The Mia Farrow/Soon Yi escapade threw you for a loop, but you still adore the self deprecating, bespectacled red head? We'll let you in on a secret — every Monday Mr. Allen plays the clarinet in a band that performs at the Cafe Carlyle. The setting is very intimate — performers are practically sitting in the audience's lap — which is great for Eartha Kitt fans that want to hear her cat growl up close. Or catch the ever-endearing Bobby Short as he tears into his 33rd year at the Cafe.

Type of Establishment
Cafe/Live Music

Hours
M-Sa 8:45pm,
          10:45pm

Drink Prices
$$$$

Food
International

Nearest Subway
6 to 77th Street

Credit Cards
MC,V,AmEx

$50 Cover
Charge

Club Macanudo
26 EAST 63RD STREET
BETWEEN PARK & MADISON
(212) 752-8200

Filled with intricate hardwood, comfortable couches, and velvet chairs, this classy cigar lounge and restaurant has spared no expense when it comes to decoration and ambiance. Offering a selection of over 130 cigars from around the world, private humidors and cigar school every Monday, this is the place to come if you're an aspiring cigar aficionado. Though the menu and drinks are pricey, a state-of-the-art ventilation system keeps the visibility and breathability level high. Frequented by cigar lovers from around the city (mostly male), the relaxing environs make for a sophisticated evening out on the town. Note: Jacket required.

Type of Establishment
Bar/Restaurant

Hours
M-T 4pm-
          12:30am
W-F 4pm-1:30am
Sa 5pm-1:30am

Drink Prices
$$$$

Food
American Bistro

Nearest Subway
B,Q to Lexington Avenue

Credit Cards
All Major

DT-UT

1626 2ND AVENUE
BETWEEN 84TH & 85TH STREET
(212)327-1327

Type of Establishment
Cafe

Hours
Su-Th 7:30am-
12am
F-Sa 8:30am-
2am

Drink Prices
$$

Food
Desserts

Nearest Subway
4,5,6 to
86th Street

Credit Cards
Cash Only

It's Monday night, you're sitting at home on the Upper East Side, and you can't figure out where to meet a friend for a quick chat and espresso ... Or you're looking for that perfect couch to wind down a date over a glass of wine ... Or even just out to grab a quick chocolate cake fix? You'll all find a niche here to meet your mellow-night standards. With an international list of beers, wines and ports, and a full selection of sweets and cafe creations, DT-UT will keep you busy as you paddle away at your lap-top or share a delicious Rice Krispy treat.

Hi-Life Restaurant & Lounge

1340 1ST AVENUE @ 72ND STREET
(212) 249-3600

Type of Establishment
Bar/Restaurant

Hours
Su-W 11:30am-
1:30am
Th-Sa 11:30am-
3am

Drink Prices
$$

Food
Eclectic

Nearest Subway
6 to Hunter
College

Credit Cards
All Major

Just when you thought you'd escaped the flashy neon store fronts that pollute Times Square, just when you thought people were sooo over the 80s giant aquariums that were in every *Miami Vice* episode, just when you thought a place on the Upper East Side would never even go there, Hi-Life went there, fish tank, neon sign and all. A little gaudy? Yeah. A lot of fun? Definitely. The restaurant is kid friendly in the early evening but after the rug rats have been tucked in, mommy and daddy meet up with their friends, sip martinis, and stuff themselves silly.

Lexington Bar and Books

1020 LEXINGTON AVENUE @ 73RD STREET
(212) 717-3902

Type of Establishment
Bar

Hours
M-Th 4:30pm-
2am
F-Sa 5:30pm-
4am
Su 6pm-2am

Drink Prices
$$$

Food
N/A

Nearest Subway
6 to 77th Street

Credit Cards
MC,V,AmEx

We think it apropos that Lexington Bar and Books is right next door to an actual bookstore. Presumably, if you found yourself dissatisfied with their library, it would only take a minute to purchase your own pulp fiction. Unlike it's older brother down on Hudson Street, this Bar and Books is far bigger and lacks that Village edge — no sneakers, no caps, and shirts must have a collar. Most of the clientele are captains of industry who are not interested in reading. They'd rather get down to business ... a club sandwich, a strong cigar and a potent martini to wash it all down.

Manny's Car Wash
1558 3RD AVENUE
BETWEEN 87TH & 88TH STREET
(212) 369-BLUE

It's not a car wash. And it's not a strip club although the bright flashing lights around the marquee are reminiscent of places where men yell, "give me hooters." Manny's Car Wash serves up none of that. No boobs, no lube, just blues and plenty of it seven nights a week. How anything more than a harmonica can fit on the small corner stage is a mystery, but the band starts at 9:30 p.m. and the place is always crowded with uptowners, citywide blues enthusiasts and out-of-towners looking for a down-home good time.

Type of Establishment
Blues Bar

Hours
Su-Th 5pm-
　2:30am
F-Sa 5pm-4am

Drink Prices
$$

Food
N/A

Nearest Subway
4,5,6 to
86th Street

Credit Cards
All Major

Martell's
1469 3RD AVENUE @ 83RD STREET
(212) 879-1717

Martell's is the Upper East Side's version of the neighborhood diner but the continental American fare tastes and looks a lot better. Employees work and play together, patrons work and play with employees, it's one big happy family where regulars like Maria from Korea, Squiggy, and Murphy even have their names engraved in brass plates on the bar. Newcomers may feel like they're encroaching on the 'in crowd,' but after multiple drinks and some crab cakes, you'll be making plans to head out to Fairfield County with one of them soon enough.

Type of Establishment
Bar/Restaurant

Hours
Daily 12pm-4am

Drink Prices
$$

Food
American

Nearest Subway
4,5,6 to
86th Street

Credit Cards
All Major

Merchants NY
1125 1ST AVENUE @ 62ND STREET
(212) 832-1551

Why waste your night journeying to a trendy bar for pre-dinner drinks, on to an elegant restaurant for dinner and then to a sexy jazz lounge for after-dinner drinks and cigars, when you can do all that and more in one place? Merchants is one-stop shopping and shifting from one part of the evening to another is as effortless as walking a couple of steps. The moderately priced menu is American cuisine with a Merchant twist — in other words, it too has a lot of different things to offer.

Type of Establishment
Bar/Restaurant/
Lounge

Hours
M-F 5pm-4am
Sa-Su 11:30am-
　4am

Drink Prices
$$

Food
American

Nearest Subway
4,5,6 to
59th Street

Credit Cards
All Major

Tar Bar

1412 1ST AVENUE
BETWEEN 74TH & 75TH STREET
(212) 570-5704

While candle shadows dance on the wall, Barry White croons in the background, singles mingle effortlessly at the bar, old friends catch-up while playing pool, and first dates get to know each other better in the booths. The Tar Bar caters to an older set (veterans of the disco era who've still got a little boogie in them) but mature Gen Xers are welcome. The place has got the kind of class that money can't buy and the staff, from owner Vincent on down, has a refreshing 'mi casa es su casa' type attitude.

Type of Establishment
Bar

Hours
M-Th 5pm-2am
F-Sa 5pm-4am

Drink Prices
$$

Food
Bar Menu

Nearest Subway
6 to 77th Street

Credit Cards
All Major

Trilogy Bar & Grill

1403 2ND AVENUE @ 73RD STREET
(212) 794-1870

If this bar were downtown it'd have peanut shells on the floor and neon bar signs haphazardly hung on the walls. But Trilogy is on the Upper East Side so the floor is spotless, framed pictures hang perfectly, and instead of Chex Mix you have a complete and extremely affordable menu which ranges from fried calamari to mesculan salad. Though one wouldn't expect it from a bar that has more than its fair share of cardigan and khaki wearing yuppies, Trilogy has the recipe for a cheap good time. Guessing heads or tails correctly on Flip Night Tuesday wins you a free drink.

Type of Establishment
Bar/Restaurant

Hours
Su-Th 5pm-2am
F-Sa 5pm-4am

Drink Prices
$$

Food
American

Nearest Subway
6 to 77th Street

Credit Cards
All Major

MIDTOWN WEST

Midtown West is a glitter-splashed stroll down Broadway through the Theater District and into the illuminated capital of commercialism that is Times Square.

These images of midtown are how the rest of the world sees Manhattan, but the area has so much more to offer. A refined taste of the New York City high life, authentic as well as pre-fabricated — and not always as polished as you may think. Midtown West nightlife ranges from the ultra-sophistication of the Oak Room to the swanky Swing 46 and Flute.

Though the theater is the centerpiece of this neighborhood, it's far from the only option. Experience the thrill of court-side seats at Madison Square Garden and the throngs of ravenous, blood-thirsty fans. Then try the awe-inspiring Intrepid Sea, Air and Space Museum. The car and boat shows at the Jacob Javitz Convention Center. A sight-seeing tour around Manhattan aboard the Circle Line. There is an endless list of things to do both night and day.

The unmistakable eye in this swirling neon storm of excitement is Times Square. Having undergone a major face lift recently, the world-renowned crossroads is more inviting than ever for nightlife and theatergoers alike. Close and careful attention must be paid to selecting just the right pre- or post-theater dining experience. Should it be celebrity spotting at Sardi's, or dinner and dancing at an exclusive supper club? Perhaps a small side-order of comedy with your evening, sir? It's all here for the taking.

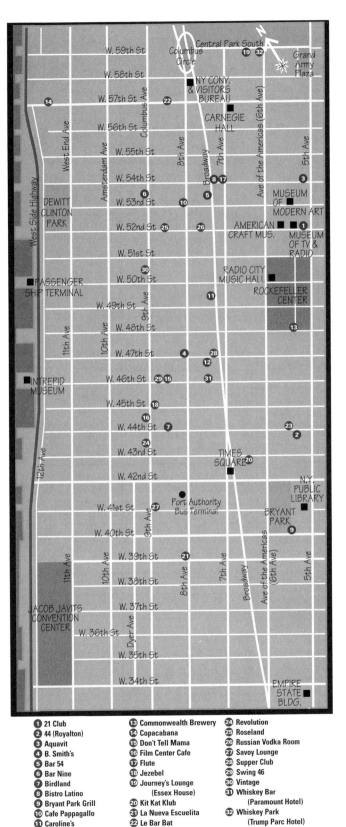

1. 21 Club
2. 44 (Royalton)
3. Aquavit
4. B. Smith's
5. Bar 54
6. Bar Nine
7. Birdland
8. Bistro Latino
9. Bryant Park Grill
10. Cafe Pappagallo
11. Caroline's
12. China Club
13. Commonwealth Brewery
14. Copacabana
15. Don't Tell Mama
16. Film Center Cafe
17. Flute
18. Jezebel
19. Journey's Lounge (Essex House)
20. Kit Kat Klub
21. La Nueva Escuelita
22. Le Bar Bat
23. Oak Room (Algonquin Hotel)
24. Revolution
25. Roseland
26. Russian Vodka Room
27. Savoy Lounge
28. Supper Club
29. Swing 46
30. Vintage
31. Whiskey Bar (Paramount Hotel)
32. Whiskey Park (Trump Parc Hotel)

21 Club

21 WEST 52ND STREET
BETWEEN 5TH & 6TH AVENUE
(212) 582-7200

The navy-blue suits, white shirts and wing-tips that abound are the first hints that the clientele at the 21 Club is very well-heeled. "We get a lot of the *Fortune 500* type," said a general manager of the multilevel restaurant that's been around since 1929. With ten function rooms, approximately 15,000 bottles of wine, a museum of pre-embargo Cuban cigars and a menu that features New American cuisine, it's clear to see why the good ol' boy network loves this place ... (but we also think they like playing with the toy trucks and model planes that hang from the ceiling).

Type of Establishment
Bar/Restaurant

Hours
Daily 5:30pm-11pm

Drink Prices
$$$$

Food
New American

Nearest Subway
B,D,F,Q to Rockefeller Center

Credit Cards
All Major

Jacket & Tie

44 (Royalton)

44 WEST 44TH STREET
BETWEEN 5TH & 6TH AVENUE
(212) 944-8844

This wonderfully unconventional and smart hotel lounge/restaurant/bar, designed by the unbeatable French architect, Philippe Starck, is a très European mix of welcoming comfort and nonchalant style. The elongated lounge, submerged into the hotel lobby, feels like a reversed fashion catwalk. Beautiful people in European designer clothes, guys with pony-tails and middle-aged hotel guests, who sink into designer chairs, give this place a relaxed, drop-by cocktail party feel. Sneak around the corner to the Vodka & Champagne bar, upholstered in floor-to-ceiling leather, for an exotic array of forbidden vodkas.

Type of Establishment
Bar/Restaurant

Hours
Su-Th 6pm-11pm
F-Sa 6pm-12am

Drink Prices
$$$$

Food
New American

Nearest Subway
B,D,F,Q to 42nd Street

Credit Cards
MC,V,AmEx

Aquavit

13 WEST 54TH STREET
BETWEEN 5TH & 6TH AVENUE
(212) 307-7311

"I'm in the mood for some herring" is not a phrase that one hears often. But after a trip to Aquavit, the sleek Scandinavian restaurant across the street from the Museum of Modern Art, dishes like Swedish bouillabaisse will be as inviting to your palate as grandma's apple pie. The only thing more intoxicating than the food and assortment of flavored Aquavits (the national drink of Scandinavia made of potato vodka) is the atmosphere in the atrium, featuring a two-story-high waterfall and a sun (and star) gulping skylight.

Type of Establishment
Bar/Restaurant

Hours
Daily 5pm-12am

Drink Prices
$$$$

Food
Scandinavian

Nearest Subway
E,F to 5th Avenue

Credit Cards
All Major

B. Smith's

771 8TH AVENUE @ 47TH STREET
(212) 247-2222

Despite popular belief, this is not a soul food restaurant. While grandma's cooking up smothered chicken and cornbread someplace else, B. Smith's is perfecting a simply roasted breast of chicken, rubbed with herbs and shallots ($13.95). Mmmmm. A little hoity toity, yes, but the restaurant is in the heart of the Theater District and the Broadway-goers and buppies that regularly stream through wouldn't have it any other way.

Type of Establishment
Bar/Restaurant

Hours
Daily 12pm-11:30pm

Drink Prices
$$$

Food
Eclectic

Nearest Subway
C,E to 50th Street

Credit Cards
All Major

Bar 54

1701 BROADWAY
BETWEEN 53RD & 54TH STREET
(212) 247-0720

Located right in the midst of the Theater District and next to the David Letterman Show, Bar 54 has a tough act to follow. Crowded with pre- and post-theater crowds and the corporates from the neighborhood, this 'run of the mill' American bar/restaurant can be a nice respite from the glitz and glamour that surrounds it. Offering a full dining room with an American menu, international cigar selection, and live jazz nearly every night of the week, Bar 54 fits the bill for a quicky in a neighborhood where options are at a premium.

Type of Establishment
Bar/Restaurant

Hours
Daily 11am-2am

Drink Prices
$$$

Food
Italian/American

Nearest Subway
B,D,E to 7th Avenue

Credit Cards
All Major

Bar Nine

807 9TH AVENUE
BETWEEN 53RD & 54TH STREET
(212) 399-9336

Here's a cozy midtown lounge without the midtown attitude. What began as a neighborhood watering hole now attracts regulars from all over the city, and for good reason. Featured on the *Montel Williams Show* for a segment on popular singles bars, Bar Nine is a good place to meet that someone new or get that someone old off your mind. Seating in the main lounge encourages communal interaction. The kitchen closes at midnight so order early. Note: Management prides itself on its martinis, so make sure you tell them what you think.

Type of Establishment
Restaurant/Lounge

Hours
Daily 4:30pm-4am

Drink Prices
$$$

Food
American

Nearest Subway
C,E to 50th Street

Credit Cards
MC,V,AmEx

Type of Establishment
Live Music

Hours
M-Sa 5pm-3am
Su 12pm-3am

Drink Prices
$$$

Food
Continental

Nearest Subway
A,C,E to
42nd Street

Credit Cards
All Major

Birdland

315 WEST 44TH STREET
BETWEEN 8TH & 9TH AVENUE
(212) 581-3080

Enjoy serious jazz by national headliners and internationally established artists at this cool, spacious jazz Mecca. The centerpiece here is great live music, so the big, theater-like stage is visible from all the leveled tables as well as from the casual bar area. The middle-aged, mostly white crowd of jazz freaks, artists, intellectuals and tourists, in relaxed but upscale outfits, adheres to the Quiet Policy. At the concert's end, the audience awakens from its jazz stupor and drifts by the gift shop where CDs and t-shirts are sold.

Type of Establishment
Bar/Restaurant

Hours
M-Th 6pm-2am
F-Sa 6pm-4am

Drink Prices
$$$$

Food
Latin American

Nearest Subway
B,D,E to
7th Avenue

Credit Cards
All Major

Bistro Latino

1711 BROADWAY @ 54TH STREET
(212) 245-7099

"You can dine and dance in the same room, there's no need to leave here and go to a club," said the owner of Bistro Latino, a hot Latin restaurant in the heart of midtown. The food here is delicioso! Work off the Churrasco Andino and Yucca Fries ($18.95) on the dance floor, but beware, the patrons here dance until they drop … and sometimes that doesn't even stop them. For those with two left feet, there is a Thursday night salsa class that's free. But like one Bistro Latino loyalist urged, "Come in and try it, don't just read about it!"

Type of Establishment
Bar/Restaurant

Hours
Daily 11:30am-
12am

Drink Prices
$$$

Food
American

Nearest Subway
B,D,F,Q to
42nd Street

Credit Cards
All Major

Bryant Park Grill

25 WEST 40TH STREET
BETWEEN 5TH & 6TH AVENUE
(212) 840-6500

It's like being in a New York version of *Sense and Sensibility* at this light, flowery, and ivy-covered venue with wicker chairs and white umbrellas that extend from the New York Public Library into Bryant Park. Come here in the summer, hang out with your pals from work, mingle with the corporate single scene at the cafe or watch the park's outdoor movies while having a snack from the light menu on the rooftop. If it gets too hot (or cold, in the winter), opt for the temperate bar that resides underneath a pastel painting of cheerful birds in yellow and blue.

Cafe Pappagallo

891 8TH AVENUE @ 53RD STREET
(212) 956-6000

What will it be tonight? Peanut Butter and Jelly martini, Bikini martini or a traditional Naked martini? With over 101 different martinis on the menu it may take you a while to decide. Sit back and take your time as the busy sights and sounds of 8th Avenue flood in from the open plate glass doors. The golden-hued ceiling reflecting soft candlelight comforts you whether lounging at the bar or enjoying the house special: Lobster Ravioli. Walking distance from the Theater District, Cafe Pappagallo is ideal for both corporate and intimate encounters.

Type of Establishment
Bar/Restaurant

Hours
Su-Th 4pm-12am
F-Sa 4pm-1am

Drink Prices
$$

Food
Italian

Nearest Subway
B,D,E to 7th Avenue

Credit Cards
All Major

Caroline's

1626 BROADWAY
BETWEEN 49TH & 50TH STREET
(212) 956-0101

If your funny bone has been in need of some attention, Caroline's has just the remedy. This midtown comedy club, right next to the Comedy Nation restaurant, is a laugh a minute. The semi-circular room ensures that patrons get a good view of the stage that's featured everyone from Whoopi Goldberg to Seinfeld. The cover is usually between $10-$20 in addition to a two drink minimum. Two shows a night, three on the weekends. Don't choke on your french fries or buffalo wings, you might die laughing.

Type of Establishment
Restaurant/ Comedy Club

Hours
Su-Th 7:30pm, 9:30pm
F-Sa 8pm, 10:30pm, 12:30am

Drink Prices
$$$

Food
American

Nearest Subway
1,9 to 50th Street

Credit Cards
All Major

China Club

268 WEST 47TH STREET
BETWEEN 7TH & 8TH AVENUE
(212) 398-3800

A longtime staple of uptown Manhattan nightlife known especially for its Monday night industry parties, the China Club has moved that flavor into midtown opening up a location that is part upscale restaurant and part mature nightclub. The Pan-Asian menu features delicacies including Katafi-wrapped tiger shrimp and five spice crusted loin of sushi tuna, served in an elegant candle-lit atmosphere. The evenings belong to the nightclub that features a polished dance floor, live entertainment and three fully-stocked bars, including freezers for vodka to make that perfect martini or Cosmopolitan.

Type of Establishment
Restaurant/Club

Hours
M-Sa 10pm-4am

Drink Prices
$$$$

Food
Pan-Asian

Nearest Subway
C,E to 50th Street

Credit Cards
All Major

Commonwealth Brewery

35 WEST 48TH STREET
BETWEEN 5TH & 6TH AVENUE
(212) 977-2269

"Let no one thirst for lack of real ale,"
the sign above the counter reads through
the floor-to-ceiling window as you approach
this midtown brewery from Rockefeller
Center. Indeed, the ale produced here in the
huge, visible beer vats is delicious. This all-
American, functionally bright and spacious
bar attracts a corporate business as well as
a tourist crowd and gets busy early during
weeknights. Have a beer and a burger
and follow a football game on one of the
many TVs.

Copacabana

617 WEST 57TH STREET
BETWEEN 11TH & 12TH AVENUE
(212) 582-2672

We couldn't find any show girls the night
we hung out at the legendary Copacabana,
but there were women everywhere wearing
the dresses Barry Manilow immortalized in
his 70s classic. They may stop their blood
from flowing, but the skin tight outfits don't
stop these mamacitas from strutting their
stuff. Salsa, meringue, flamenco, you name
it, this crowd likes to do it. The dance floor
is always pumping with energy and no one
stops shaking their bundas until the last
song is through.

Don't Tell Mama

343 WEST 46TH STREET
BETWEEN 8TH & 9TH AVENUE
(212) 757-0788

This Restaurant Row cabaret with singing
waiters fills up night after night. Full-chested
women in red evening dresses, older ladies in
pearls, guys in tuxedos or relaxed Gap linen,
come from uptown, across the tunnel and
further, determined to have a great night out
in New York City. Little black tables, 20s
posters, and live saloon piano music set the
background for this very animated, bustling
theater crowd. The two cabarets feature several shows every night. Don't miss Steven
Brinberg's impersonation of Barbra Streisand
in *The Wedding Tour.*

Type of Establishment
Bar/Restaurant

Hours
M-F 11:30am-
10:30pm
Sa 12pm-9pm
Su12pm-8pm

Drink Prices
$$$

Food
American

Nearest Subway
B,D,F,Q to
Rockefeller
Center

Credit Cards
All Major

Type of Establishment
Club

Hours
T 6pm-3am
F,Sa 10pm-5am

Drink Prices
$$$

Food
N/A

Nearest Subway
A,C,B,D,1,9 to
Columbus Circle

Credit Cards
All Major

Type of Establishment
Cabaret

Hours
Daily 4pm-4am

Drink Prices
$$

Food
N/A

Nearest Subway
A,C,E to
42nd Street

Credit Cards
MC,V,AmEx

Film Center Cafe

635 9TH AVENUE
BETWEEN 44TH & 45TH STREET
(212) 262-2525

Get a perfect concoction of Hollywood glamour and Hell's Kitchen reality at this 50s diner, bar and restaurant where artists, theater types and locals mix with producers and technicians from the Film Center across the street. 20th Century Fox and Metro-Goldwyn signs tower above you in pastel colors while their films flicker across four TV screens. The music is low and allows animated conversation among the couples near the bar and the groups of friends dining in the restaurant.

Type of Establishment
Bar/Restaurant

Hours
Su-T 12pm-2am
W-Sa 12pm-4am

Drink Prices
$$

Food
New American

Nearest Subway
A,C,E to 42nd Street

Credit Cards
All Major

Flute

205 WEST 54TH STREET
BETWEEN BROADWAY & 7TH AVENUE
(212) 265-5169

This ultra-chic midtown champagne lounge still retains the mysterious allure of the notorious speakeasy it was during prohibition, yet complimented now with an undeniable uptown 90s accent. Relax on the luxurious thick blue-velvet couches and select from the more than 105 champagnes including 15 by the glass. The early crowd, including top executives in banking and publishing, gives way to the late-night downtown trendy set after 11 p.m. A hidden recess in the floor, once used for stashing champagne during prohibition and uncovered during renovation, now holds a bottle of coveted 1928 Krug champagne covered by glass for display.

Type of Establishment
Lounge

Hours
M-Sa 5pm-4am

Drink Prices
$$$$

Food
Appetizers

Nearest Subway
B,D,E to 7th Avenue

Credit Cards
All Major

Jezebel

630 9TH AVENUE @ 45TH STREET
(212) 582-1045

Hell's Kitchen's best-kept secret is as exquisite, poised and perplexing as the woman you'd want to fall in love with. A generous, inspired and unusual soul decorated this spacious locale with swings, Baccarat crystal chandeliers, French posters and shawls hanging from the ceiling. Jezebel attracts characters from the theater, business and music industries (don't be surprised to find Babyface or Oliver Stone dining here). Beautiful staff serve excellent soul food in this mellow, understated yet truly grand blend of Harlem Renaissance and pre-war France.

Type of Establishment
Bar/Restaurant

Hours
M-Th 5:30pm-
10:30pm
F-Sa 5:30pm-
1am

Drink Prices
$$$

Food
Southern/Soul

Nearest Subway
A,C,E to 42nd Street

Credit Cards
AmEx

Journey's Lounge (Essex House)

160 CENTRAL PARK SOUTH
BETWEEN 6TH & 7TH AVENUE
(212) 247-0300

Type of Establishment
Bar

Hours
Daily 12pm-12am

Drink Prices
$$$$

Food
Appetizers

Nearest Subway
N,R to 57th Street

Credit Cards
All Major

This classy old English hotel bar and its professional staff keep what they promise — to accommodate you with the perfect mix of homey coziness and stylish anonymity after a long journey. Impeccable leather sofas and upholstered chairs welcome you in this carpeted living room with a fireplace underneath paintings of aristocratic hunting scenes. Tourists, couples, friends and families have a drink or a snack at the intimately spread-out low tables. If you follow the sound of the waterfall behind the fireplace, you'll find a marvelous little winter garden.

Kit Kat Klub

124 WEST 43RD STREET
BETWEEN 6TH AVENUE & BROADWAY
(212) 819-0377

Type of Establishment
Club/Cabaret

Hours
F 9:30pm-4am
Sa-Su 10:30am-4am

Drink Prices
$$$$

Food
N/A

Nearest Subway
1,2,3,9 to 42nd Street

Credit Cards
All Major

The sign out front reads, "In here life is beautiful." The young multi-culti crowd extends down the block. They're tired of waiting and anxious to get in. They can hear the music blaring and they all want a piece of the Kit Kat. Some nights, it's a giant club filled with partygoers intoxicated by the bright lights, booming system, and giant disco balls. Other nights, it's a cabaret or Broadway theatre house. May we suggest the skybox upstairs — it has a service bar and comfortable leopard covered couches.

La Nueva Escuelita

301 WEST 39TH STREET @ 8TH AVENUE
(212) 631-0588

Type of Establishment
Club

Hours
Th-Su 10pm-5am

Drink Prices
$$$

Food
N/A

Nearest Subway
A,C,E to 42nd Street

Credit Cards
Cash Only

Do you like to rumba with drag princesses and gay salseros in pleated pants as they spin into each other's arms? Misogynist Chelsea boys a few blocks south could learn something at this Latin school for the art of seduction, even though it happens just between machos. The artistry on the pulsating dance floor is attentively watched by the chicos at the bar of this dimly lit, mirrored underground, if they're not busy sticking dollar bills into the compact bailerino's only piece of clothing — his underwear. There are also sexy mamacitas and hardy dikes who enjoy Latin and house sounds without being hassled.

Le Bar Bat

311 WEST 57TH STREET
BETWEEN 8TH & 9TH AVENUE
(212) 307-7228

This chic spot, designed to appear as a bat cave, adorned with blue-tinged bat-shaped lights, draws one of the most interesting crowds in midtown. Prepare yourself though, because the crowd is young, the energy is high and the room is loud. If the high-octane energy upstairs is just not enough for you, then swoop downstairs into the lower lounge and dance the night away.

Type of Establishment
Bar/Restaurant/Club

Hours
Daily 5pm-4am

Drink Prices
$$$

Food
American

Nearest Subway
A,C,B,D,1,9 to Columbus Circle

Credit Cards
All Major

Oak Room (Algonquin Hotel)

59 WEST 44TH STREET
BETWEEN 5TH & 6TH AVENUE
(212) 840-6800

The famed Algonquin's oak-paneled lobby is an ideal setting for congregation. Long considered Manhattan's oasis of civility, its hallowed walls once echoed the intellectual debates of such literary luminaries as William Faulkner, Sinclair Lewis, James Thurber and countless others. Velvet overstuffed sofas and chairs provide a sophisticated yet comfortable environment. Enjoy a cocktail in the plush lobby or step into the Oak Room for continental cuisine served in an elegant atmosphere featuring live piano, opera, cabaret entertainment and literary readings.

Type of Establishment
Restaurant/Cabaret

Hours
Daily 5pm-1am

Drink Prices
$$$$

Food
Continental

Nearest Subway
B,D,F,Q to 42nd street

Credit Cards
All Major

$35 cover
+ $15 drink min.
for shows

Revolution

611 9TH AVENUE
BETWEEN 43RD & 44TH STREET
(212) 489-8451

Downtown meets midtown in this boisterous amalgam of bar/restaurant/lounge, but thanks to its location in Hell's Kitchen, it resists snobbery. A relaxed, young and upbeat crowd, from in and out-of-town, drinks beer at the royal-size bar, dines in the spacious restaurant in the back or cuddles up in the comfortable sofas in the front as it watches 9th Avenue go by. A DJ fills the high ceilings with disco and hip-hop tunes every night. When it gets too packed on weekends, the crowd just spills over to the Avenue.

Type of Establishment
Bar/Restaurant

Hours
Daily 5pm-3am

Drink Prices
$$$

Food
Eclectic American

Nearest Subway
A,C,E to 42nd Street

Credit Cards
All Major

Roseland

239 WEST 52ND STREET
BETWEEN 8TH & 9TH AVENUE
(212) 813-9400

Type of Establishment	Live Music
Hours	Varies Daily
Drink Prices	$$$
Food	N/A
Nearest Subway	B,D,E to 7th Avenue
Credit Cards	All Major Tickets Only

This pre-war designed concert venue has seen them all and is still going strong. Its cavernous main floor has hosted some of the biggest acts in music today, as it did back in the 50s. Home to the friendliest, if not the largest mosh pit in the city, Roseland is an ideal venue to see super-charged alternative and mainstream rock bands as well as infrequent, but equally interesting events such as a tattoo convention. If you lose your breath in the pit or just need an escape from the crush of the crowd, retreat to the full back bar or downstairs and relax.

Russian Vodka Room

265 WEST 52ND STREET
BETWEEN BROADWAY & 8TH AVENUE
(212) 307-5835

Type of Establishment	Bar/Restaurant
Hours	Su-Th 4pm-2am F-Sa 4pm-4am
Drink Prices	$$$
Food	Russian
Nearest Subway	B,D,E to 7th Avenue
Credit Cards	All Major

Whether they are nostalgic immigrants from the Black Sea or just cheap vodka drinkers, most clients in this smoky, down-to-Russian-earth bar near the Theater District are regulars. Some Americans enjoy casual conversations at the bright front bar, but comrades prefer keeping secrets in the intimate back room. Try smoked veal tongue with Khvanchkara wine from Georgia, Stalin's favorite (he is still talked of in the present tense here). The Russian bartender and the music are very 80s, and the stories as outdated as Peter the Great or as current as green card lotteries.

Savoy Lounge

355 WEST 41ST STREET @ 9TH AVENUE
(212) 947-5255

Type of Establishment	Lounge/ Live Music
Hours	Daily 8am-4am
Drink Prices	$
Food	N/A
Nearest Subway	A,C,E to 42nd Street
Credit Cards	All Major

Lost between the monstrous Port Authority and Lincoln Tunnel, this little place is a real trove. Owner George Hatfield has put all his love for jazz into this intimate, smoky dive with a stage big enough to accommodate groovy bebop, jazz, blues and Latin bands every night. Mingle with authentic, unhip New Yorkers: from the lonely old-timer with his cowboy hat drawn over his face, to the lively aspiring actress trying to smoke cigars. Let yourself be taken by George's whims, such as real-life plays with street action or free Sunday buffets cooked up by him and his staff.

Supper Club

240 WEST 47TH STREET
BETWEEN 8TH AVENUE & BROADWAY
(212) 921-1940

This joint is jumpin'. The soulful siren is sweating and singing "while you were stepping out, someone was stepping in." Members of her 17-piece big band have moved their act from the stage into the crowd. The dance floor is filled with young and old people twirling, dipping, shimmying, and barely breathing. It feels like a 40s Cotton Club, but it's a 90s Supper Club. "We're not looking to create something new, we're trying to recreate something people forgot about," said Anthony the general manager. Guess it don't mean a thing if it ain't got that swing.

Type of Establishment
Supper Club

Hours
F-Sa 5:30pm-4am

Drink Prices
$$$$

Food
Continental

Nearest Subway
B,D,F,Q to 47th-50th Street

Credit Cards
All Major

Swing 46

349 WEST 46TH STREET
BETWEEN 8TH & 9TH AVENUE
(212) 262-9554

The exuberant crowd at this throbbing 40s ballroom offers a nice change to NY's lounge scene. Here you will find rosy-cheeked swing zealots of all ages trying out steps on or behind the dance floor — their enthusiastic energy is contagious. If you're intimidated by the guys in zoot suits and suspenders flinging the girls in short dance dresses over their knees, don't worry — after a few dance classes, offered every night by Dance Manhattan, you will be able to do the same. During intermission, refresh yourself at the pink cloth-covered tables or at the bright, relaxed bar in the front.

Type of Establishment
Supper Club

Hours
Daily 12pm-4am

Drink Prices
$$$

Food
French Bistro/Italian

Nearest Subway
A,C,E to 42nd Street

Credit Cards
MC,V,AmEx

Vintage

753 9TH AVENUE
BETWEEN 50TH & 51ST STREET
(212) 581-4655

The lounge crusade has finally reached midtown's stand-offish westside — Vintage is living proof. Set in cool, 90s beige minimalism, Vintage's decor features a wild mix of styles — turn-of-the-century chaise lounges, art deco chairs, small 90s tables with candles, curtains and gold-framed mirrors. The crowd is authentic: Latinos from the neighborhood, a young downtown and entertainment crowd, gays, middle-aged groups of friends and couples, mingle here to an unusual mix of German rock, English punk and disco music.

Type of Establishment
Bar/Restaurant

Hours
Daily 11am-4am

Drink Prices
$$$

Food
American

Nearest Subway
C,E to 50th Street

Credit Cards
All Major

Type of Establishment
Bar

Hours
M-Th 4pm-4am
Sa-Su 3pm-4am

Drink Prices
$$$$

Food
N/A

Nearest Subway
1,2,3,9 to
42nd Street

Credit Cards
All Major

Whiskey Bar (Paramount Hotel)
235 WEST 46TH STREET
BETWEEN BROADWAY & 8TH AVENUE
(212) 819-0404

It may be a bar in a hotel, but this is not your typical hotel bar. Emerging as a popular destination for the pre- and post-theater scene, this spot is littered with friendly tourists, suits and suburbanites. As they only seat two to a table, it's a good spot to bring that significant other, or join the crowd at the bar for either the after-work or late-night rushes. If you're not one of the lucky few who snagged a coveted barstool, relax in one of the couches or chairs strewn about. Arrive early and you may avoid having to wait on line.

Type of Establishment
Bar

Hours
Su-T 4pm-2am
W-Sa 4pm-4am

Drink Prices
$$$$

Food
N/A

Nearest Subway
A,C,B,D,1,9 to
Columbus Circle

Credit Cards
All Major

Whiskey Park (Trump Parc Hotel)
100 CENTRAL PARK SOUTH @ 6TH AVENUE
(212) 307-9222

Professionals and tourists like to have a smooth whiskey to soft rock in this dark brown, velvety venue among the noble Central Park South hotels, as they sink into the comfortable leather couches or the cushions on the window sills, and watch the horse carriages disappear in the park outside. Guys in white pants and dark jackets check out dressed-up girlfriends, as far as possible in this dimly lit, neat and chic bar with black and white photographs, while groups of friends enjoy themselves at the larger tables.

MIDTOWN EAST

AND CENTRAL
TER...

From its posh, elegant hotels to the elaborate shopping Mecca along Fifth Avenue, Midtown East exudes the finest Manhattan has to offer — albeit slightly pretentious and certainly expensive.

Visitors to the area are conspicuous — dodging in and out between rogue taxis, with craned necks straining to look up at the majestic skyscrapers. The area offers endless sightseeing opportunities, including the Empire State Building, FAO Schwartz, Grand Central Terminal, Radio City Music Hall, St. Patrick's Cathedral, Trump Tower, the United Nations. A crisp afternoon of ice skating at Rockefeller Center before treating yourself to a ridiculously expensive shopping spree at Bergdorf's and Saks is the typical holiday, but the options extend far beyond the confines of tourist traps. You'll probably run out of time and money before things to do.

Stroll down east of 3rd Avenue and see how the other half lives in the cozy and urban upper-crusty bistros and cigar lounges in Kips Bay, Murray Hill and Sutton Place. Walk further towards the river and behold the majesty of the United Nations complex, just don't expect to find any parking here.

Nightlife in Midtown East is a well rehearsed orchestra of hotel bars, theme clubs, champagne lounges, supper clubs, pre- and post-theater dining — just a sampling of the finest sophistication New York City has to offer. Whether it's a business meeting or an intimate dinner, there is an endless number of ideal situations to make that desired impression.

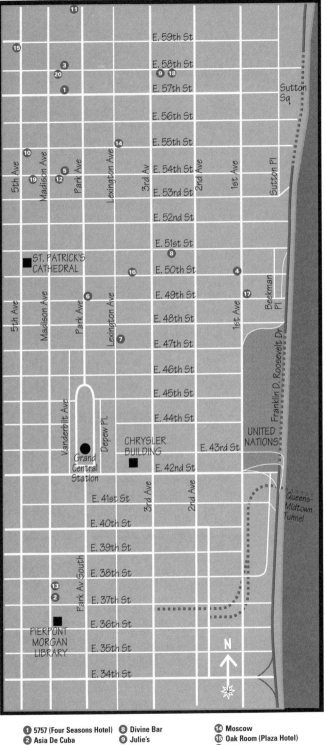

1. 5757 (Four Seasons Hotel)
2. Asia De Cuba
3. Au Bar
4. Beekman Bar and Books
5. Bill's Gay Nineties
6. Bull & Bear
   (Waldorf-Astoria)
7. Denim & Diamonds
8. Divine Bar
9. Julie's
10. King Cole Bar
    (St. Regis Hotel)
11. Match-Uptown
12. Monkey Bar
    (Hotel Elysee)
13. Morgan's
    (Morgan Hotel)
14. Moscow
15. Oak Room (Plaza Hotel)
16. Tatou
17. Top of the Tower
18. The Townhouse
19. Typhoon Brewery
20. The Web

5757 (Four Seasons Hotel)

57 EAST 57TH STREET
BETWEEN PARK & MADISON
(212) 758-5757

Type of Establishment
Bar/Restaurant

Hours
M-Sa 3:30pm-1am
Su 3:30pm-12am

Drink Prices
$$$$

Food
New American

Nearest Subway
4,5,6,N,R to 59th Street

Credit Cards
All Major

Whether it's for an intimate rendezvous, business lunch or pre-theater dining, 5757 offers a taste of Manhattan's high life. After all, located in the lobby of the Four Seasons Hotel anything less would seem drastically out of place. The art deco design features a ceiling of Danish beechwood panel, bronze chandeliers and deep cherry floors with mahogany inlays. Live jazz provides the appropriate soothing sounds for this masterpiece. It is appropriately expensive, so plan for the occasion.

Asia De Cuba

237 MADISON AVENUE
BETWEEN 37TH & 38TH STREET
(212) 726-7755

Type of Establishment
Bar/Restaurant

Hours
Su-Th 5:30pm-11:30pm
F-Sa 5:30pm-1am

Drink Prices
$$$$

Food
Asian/Cuban

Nearest Subway
4,5,6,7 to Grand Central

Credit Cards
All Major

Housed in the same art deco building as the Morgan Hotel, this blend of colonial Spanish and Asian chic reveals the ultimate taste in interior design and cuisine. The bright duplex, set against a halcyon image of a tropical waterfall, playfully combines bar, lounge and restaurant. Entertainment and corporate figures have drinks in leather rocking chairs surrounded by African art and world music. Dine along the gallery's glass railings that allow for eying the banquet below at the elongated, illuminated marble table. Semicircular couches accommodate private groups, and glass shelves expose drinks made from 36 different rums.

Au Bar

41 EAST 58TH STREET
BETWEEN PARK & MADISON
(212) 308-9455

Type of Establishment
Lounge/Club

Hours
Daily 9pm-4am

Drink Prices
$$$$

Food
Continental

Nearest Subway
4,5,6,N,R to 59th Street

Credit Cards
MC,V,AmEx

$10-$25 Cover

Whether you're looking to dance or just browse, get past the velvet rope and you're in for a good night. This amalgam of styles, nationalities and pick-up lines has long endured the trials of New York nightlife. Whether it's the long narrow bar that leaves you no choice but to press flesh and strike a conversation or the packed dance floor that grooves to past and present dance favorites, you can find satisfaction somewhere in the mix. Open all week, the atmosphere becomes more clublike as the weekend approaches; however, they up the ante as well.

Beekman Bar and Books

889 1ST AVENUE @ 50TH STREET
(212) 980-9314

Ease into this classy yet cozy New England cigar bar below street level and engage in an animated conversation or relax with a book near the fireplace. Fine wood trimmings, bookshelves, and comfortable couches recreate the intimate and welcoming atmosphere of New York's 40s and 50s hotel bars. A professional bartender in a bow tie serves up cocktails and cigars to an upscale crowd that ranges from midtown suits, locals from the Upper East Side and international civil servants from the nearby United Nations. All this amongst the sounds of sophisticated jazz, bebop, Latin and European tunes.

Type of Establishment
Bar

Hours
M-Th 4:30pm-2am
F-Sa 4:30pm-4am
Su 6pm-2am

Drink Prices
$$$

Food
N/A

Nearest Subway
6 to 51st Street

Credit Cards
All Major

Jacket & Tie

Bill's Gay Nineties

57 EAST 54TH STREET
BETWEEN PARK & MADISON
(212) 355-0243

That's Nineties — as in 1890s. Step into this popular former prohibition-era speakeasy and sample the shadows of an era long past, yet imbedded in the foundation of Manhattan's nightlife. Wall-to-wall period pictures of athletes and personalities — including signed prints of exhibits at the 1893 Columbia World's Fair in Chicago — peer down at you as you enjoy your dinner or drinks. The second floor dining room comes alive with the soulful sounds of Dixieland jazz on Monday nights, and features live cabaret talent Tuesday through Saturday.

Type of Establishment
Bar/Restaurant

Hours
M-Sa 11:30am-1am

Drink Prices
$$$

Food
American

Nearest Subway
E,F to
3rd Avenue

Credit Cards
All Major

Bull & Bear (Waldorf-Astoria)

301 PARK AVENUE @ 49TH STREET
(212) 872-4900

Located in the heart of the Waldorf-Astoria Hotel, this bar/restaurant, named after the highs and lows of the stock market, is clearly all about business. Oil paintings of horses, upholstered couches and brown leather chairs give B&B a striking resemblance to a grandfather's study (there's even a mini-library). A bit boring yes, but the excitement comes from knowing that in different corners of the room men named Thurston the III and Chip are making million-dollar deals over wine, cigars and Black Angus steaks ($30).

Type of Establishment
Bar/Restaurant

Hours
Daily 12pm-11:30pm

Drink Prices
$$$$

Food
American

Nearest Subway
E,F to
3rd Avenue

Credit Cards
All Major

Denim & Diamonds

Type of Establishment
Bar/Restaurant

Hours
Daily 7pm-4am

Drink Prices
$$$

Food
American

Nearest Subway
4,5,6,7 to Grand Central

Credit Cards
All Major

511 LEXINGTON AVENUE
BETWEEN 47TH & 48TH STREET
(212) 371-1600

Step off a midtown street into the heart of a polished Midwest honky-tonk where the walls are outfitted with cowboy trimmings. Saddle up to the upstairs bar to whet your whistle, then mosey on down to the lower dance club for a little Texas two-step. Here's the place to show off all those fancy line dances you've worked so hard at in front of the mirror. For the novice, though, they offer regular professional dance classes. You'll do better here with an oversized cowboy hat with matching spurs, but it's not required. A great place to take the lil' lady. Happy trails.

Divine Bar

Type of Establishment
Wine Bar

Hours
M-F 5pm-2am
Sa-Su 7pm-2am

Drink Prices
$$$

Food
Eclectic Tapas

Nearest Subway
6 to 51st Street

Credit Cards
MC,V,AmEx

244 EAST 51ST STREET
BETWEEN 2ND & 3RD AVENUE
(212) 319-9463

Ix-nay on the screwdrivers. Divine is within 500 feet of a synagogue so only wine and beer is served in this funky duplex townhouse. In spite of its midtown location, surprisingly this place has a strong SoHo feel — zebra-skinned chairs and rugs, orange walls, red velvet and black leather couches, candles and more candles. This place is perfect for the young, hot and powerful. Don't you dare leave without trying some of the tantalizing tapas. Mmmm…now you know why it's called "Divine."

Julie's

Type of Establishment
Bar

Hours
Daily 5pm-4am

Drink Prices
$$

Food
N/A

Nearest Subway
4,5,6,N,R to 59th Street

Credit Cards
Cash Only

204 EAST 58TH STREET
BETWEEN 2ND & 3RD AVENUE
(212) 688-1294

Men, if you're looking for that special someone you won't find her in here. Women, if you're desperately seeking Susan, walk on in and feast your eyes on Julie's smorgasbord of ladies. Like Townhouse (the gentleman's gay bar next door), this lesbian hot spot attracts a more upscale, working professional crowd. Every third Monday of the month, Personal Personals, a dating service for "wimmin," hosts a matchmaking party that's only $3 with a flyer. Don't worry about a come-on line — hostess Sonoma and her Cupid cohorts pass notes along for you shy girls.

King Cole Bar (St. Regis Hotel)
2 EAST 55TH STREET
BETWEEN MADISON & 5TH AVENUE
(212) 339-6721

Located in the lobby of the St. Regis Hotel, this elegant lounge is a taste of Old New York high society. A huge Maxfield Parrish mural of a jovial Old King Cole and his court — appraised at some $4 million — looks down upon you from behind the cherry bar, lightening the opulent atmosphere just a touch. As it should, this spot offers a wide array of brandies, champagnes, cognacs and ports. They also make an exceptional martini. Dress to impress here, and don't forget the charge cards.

Type of Establishment
Bar

Hours
Su-Th 11:30am-1am
F-Sa 11:30am-2am

Drink Prices
$$$$

Food
Hors d'oeuvres

Nearest Subway
4,5,6,N,R to 59th Street

Credit Cards
All Major

Jacket & Tie

Match-Uptown
33 EAST 60TH STREET
BETWEEN PARK & MADISON
(212) 906-9177

Though quite different from its downtown elder sibling, Match-Uptown still has the designer touch that transcends geography. Following with the same Asian-influenced menu and motif, this bar/restaurant brings a breath of fresh air to the arid canyons of Midtown East's nightlife. With a dedicated after-work crowd and a business lunch appeal, finding a seat can sometimes be a blessing. But don't let that scare you because the sushi here is too good to pass up (although you'll pay for it).

Type of Establishment
Bar/Restaurant

Hours
Su-M 11:30am-11pm
T-Sa 11am-2am

Drink Prices
$$$

Food
New American/Asian

Nearest Subway
4,5,6,N,R to 59th Street

Credit Cards
All Major

Monkey Bar (Hotel Elysee)
60 EAST 54TH STREET
BETWEEN PARK & MADISON
(212) 838-2600

While it may not draw the *Who's Who* of New York as it once did in the 40s, this piano bar with attached restaurant is certainly still a midtown gem. The dimly lit, posh oak and pale yellow decor oozes sophistication, pleasantly off-set by the wall-to-wall paintings of frolicking monkeys. Younger, upscale professionals crowd in after work, then slowly taper off as they are replaced by an older audience for the light live music. The ambiance and location are sure to impress that certain someone. The prices are a bit higher here, but worth it.

Type of Establishment
Bar/Restaurant

Hours
Daily 5:30pm-4am

Drink Prices
$$$$

Food
American

Nearest Subway
E,F to 3rd Avenue

Credit Cards
All Major

Jacket & Tie

Type of Establishment
Lounge

Hours
M-T 5pm-2am
W-Sa 5pm-4am
Su 6pm-1am

Drink Prices
$$$$

Food
N/A

Nearest Subway
4,5,6,7 to Grand Central

Credit Cards
All Major

Morgan's (Morgan Hotel)
237 MADISON AVENUE
BETWEEN 37TH & 38TH STREET
(212) 726-7600

Step down the clean stairs, past the fresh flowers and be ready for a magic marble table, diagonally shooting across the bar, illuminating its radiant patrons: the crème de la crème of the corporate and entertainment world, clad in designer suits and upscale casual wear. Smart, lean executives engage in spirited conversations in this amalgam of Old English values in a deadly stylish, cosmopolitan New York setting.

Type of Establishment
Bar/Restaurant

Hours
Daily 12pm-4am

Drink Prices
$$$$

Food
Classic Russian

Nearest Subway
E,F to
3rd Avenue

Credit Cards
All Major

Moscow
137 EAST 55TH STREET
@ LEXINGTON AVENUE
(212) 813-1313

Experience long-forgotten Russian empires, from pastoral Eastern European horse stables to sparkling czarist ballrooms lit by crystal chandeliers. Descend to the cabaret and find a colorful Russian gypsy emoting melancholy tunes, a sax player throwing kisses at comely patrons, and two roving bards singing mysterious Russian love tunes to entwined couples. Now, ascend into the cosmopolitan gallery, featuring a Russian artist's gigantic marble statues, and relax in its cool atmosphere before you venture to the blinding bright red Russian Room where fierce, painted Russian knights in metal gear and wooden Matrioshkas watch you indulge in caviar and other Russian specialties.

Type of Establishment
Bar/Restaurant

Hours
Daily 12pm-
12am

Drink Prices
$$$$

Food
American

Nearest Subway
N,R to 5th Avenue

Credit Cards
All Major

Oak Room (Plaza Hotel)
768 5TH AVENUE @ 59TH STREET
(212) 759-3000

From the high ceiling supported by massive columns to the huge plate glass windows overlooking Central Park, the Oak Room at the Plaza Hotel imposes its elegance upon you. Perhaps that is why so many tourists and businessmen favor this spot, crowding it up after work, before and after theater, and on weekends. As all successful midtown lounges should, the Oak Room features a piano bar to enjoy as you sip your overpriced martini. Note: Cigar friendly.

Tatou

151 EAST 50TH STREET
BETWEEN 3RD AVENUE & LEXINGTON
(212) 753-1144

Nestled a few blocks east from the heart of the Theater District is this comfortable upscale New Orleans-style supper club. The antique, though polished decor is a vision of traditional decadence with a deep oak finish. The circular front bar and lounge give way to the main hall where the sectioned-off seating faces the dance floor and stage. Most nights' dining entertainment includes live jazz and cabaret shows. Though the atmosphere may seem casual, dress to impress and management prefers you call ahead for reservations.

Type of Establishment
Supper Club

Hours
M-Sa 5:30pm-4am

Drink Prices
$$$

Food
Continental

Nearest Subway
6 to 51st Street

Credit Cards
All Major

Top of the Tower

3 MITCHELL PLACE
(1ST AVENUE @ 49TH STREET)
(212) 355-7300

You've found the perfect woman and you know you want to spend the rest of your life with her. You've got the ring, know exactly what you want to say to her when you pop the question, but you're looking for that perfect ultra-romantic place that's both intimate and memorable. The type of place where the moon will cast a perfect light on her face as she says, "Yes, I will marry you." Top of the Tower is that place. It's an enchanting little restaurant that serves up intimacy, American continental cuisine, delicious desserts and a breathtaking view of the East River.

Type of Establishment
Bar/Restaurant

Hours
Su-Th 5pm-1am
F-Sa 5pm-2am

Drink Prices
$$$

Food
Continental

Nearest Subway
6 to 51st Street

Credit Cards
All Major

The Townhouse

236 EAST 58TH STREET
BETWEEN 2ND & 3RD AVENUE
(212) 754-4649

It may look like a grandfather's Elk Club, but The Townhouse has got a definite (and we do mean definite) twist. "This place attracts gay men with good jobs, the type who dress well and know how to carry themselves," said a Townhouse regular. "It's very high end. It's one of most upscale gay crowds in Manhattan." He's right. You won't find any downtown drag queens or flagrant trannies here. This place leans more towards the Rock Hudson than RuPaul type. Muscle-bound bartenders, dressed in beach club chic (khaki shorts and tight aqua t-shirts) are heavy handed so the shots are grand.

Type of Establishment
Bar

Hours
Daily 4pm-4am

Drink Prices
$$$

Food
N/A

Nearest Subway
4,5,6,N,R to 59th Street

Credit Cards
All Major

Typhoon Brewery

22 EAST 54TH STREET
BETWEEN MADISON & 5TH AVENUE
(212) 754-9006

This stylish industrial brewery duplex not only surprises with its designer decor — a soothing mix of wood, metal and brick, but also with the resourceful combination of ale and Thai food. Past the impressive vats at the entrance and underneath a small, cast iron bridge is the downstairs bar. Try a Rupper Cup-winning ale and some bar food as you listen to world music. Or go upstairs and share a Thai dish, freshly cooked at the open bar/kitchen. Mingle with corporates and lawyers early on weeknights, and with a young, hipster crowd on weekends. Private rooms available.

The Web

40 EAST 58TH STREET
BETWEEN PARK & MADISON
(212) 308-1546

There are gay clubs all over the world. There are gay clubs all over New York City. But how many cities can boast of having a gay Asian club? Welcome to The Web. As the techno music booms and the strobe lights flicker, teenie-weenie, butt-huggin' briefs pump their pelvis' and strut their stuff onstage while throngs of men watch in glee. The split-level club has two bars so you can sip your beer upstairs and watch the go-go boys from the mezzanine or you can venture downstairs to the lounge and get a cage-side view.

Type of Establishment
Bar/Restaurant

Hours
M-Sa 12pm-
10pm

Drink Prices
$$$

Food
Thai

Nearest Subway
E,F to
3rd Avenue

Credit Cards
All Major

Type of Establishment
Club

Hours
M-Th 4pm-3am
F-Su 4pm-4am

Drink Prices
$$$

Food
N/A

Nearest Subway
4,5,6,N,R to
59th Street

Credit Cards
All Major

CHELSEA

A steady stream of life over the past few years has poured over Chelsea's imposing industrial landscape and forced life into its lungs.

The massive warehouses near the piers of this former shipping district are still there, but many have been reincarnated as affordable housing. Wedged between the generic rows of factories and garages now stand trendy boutiques, galleries and sidewalk eateries. The ongoing settlement of Chelsea is the story of revitalization of a once dormant gray-scale corner of Manhattan.

Chelsea's newest residents are primarily gay. In fact, many of the popular night spots springing up in the Meat Packing District along the West Side Highway reflect this northward expansion of gay culture from the West Village. This dark, gritty area lends itself to the nightlife scene, as does the large number of vacant warehouses catering to dance halls, raves, cavernous galleries and sex clubs.

Residents used to look outside the neighborhood for entertainment, but now a home-grown scene thrives — and not just on weekends. Owners and operators of numerous Chelsea bars and eateries, recognizing the potential, are constantly improving on decor and ambiance to attract neighborhood regulars. The result — a prospering nightlife, with a growing population, offering numerous unique night-crawling opportunities.

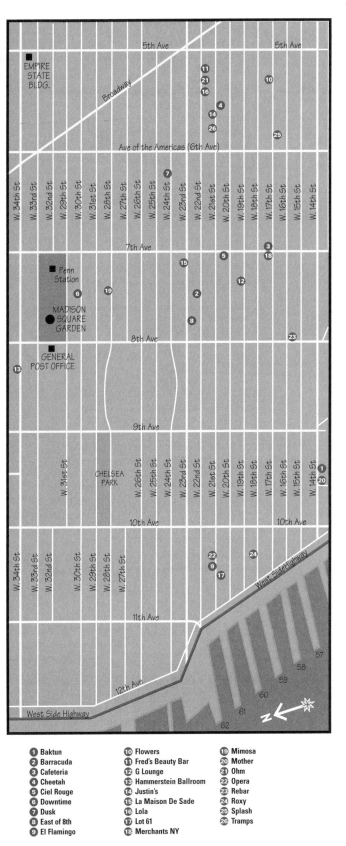

1 Baktun
2 Barracuda
3 Cafeteria
4 Cheetah
5 Ciel Rouge
6 Downtime
7 Dusk
8 East of 8th
9 El Flamingo
10 Flowers
11 Fred's Beauty Bar
12 G Lounge
13 Hammerstein Ballroom
14 Justin's
15 La Maison De Sade
16 Lola
17 Lot 61
18 Merchants NY
19 Mimosa
20 Mother
21 Ohm
22 Opera
23 Rebar
24 Roxy
25 Splash
26 Tramps

Baktun

418 WEST 14TH STREET
BETWEEN 9TH & WASHINGTON
(212) 206-1590

Located in the heart of the Meat Packing District down on 14th Street, Baktun is much more than the swanky Chelsea lounge it appears to be. Most nights the computer generated collaboration between the audio and video engineers is too enticing not to draw you in — techno-courtship between sight and sound, broadcast live over the Internet. The main lounge is the focus of the audio/visual assault, as the management has placed reduced speakers in the rear lounge making it more conducive for conversation.

Type of Establishment
Bar/Lounge

Hours
W-Sa 9pm-4am

Drink Prices
$$

Food
N/A

Nearest Subway
A,C,E to 14th Street

Credit Cards
MC,V,AmEx

baktun.com

Barracuda

275 WEST 22ND STREET
BETWEEN 7TH & 8TH AVENUE
(212) 645-8613

Sink into this dark, loud, plastique East Village-like gay dive lost on a residential Chelsea street and be ready for anything past midnight. Backpacked boys of all ages in polyester shirts order a beer from the bar with the aquarium, adjust the contents of their biker shorts, cruise around neon-lit tables and hit the pinball machine before gliding past the suggestively red pool table to the back lounge. Stay for a drag show, from Monday through Thursday, and watch the comical antics of Hedda Lettuce as 'she' quarrels with a love-sick groupie.

Type of Establishment
Bar

Hours
Daily 4pm-4am

Drink Prices
$$

Food
N/A

Nearest Subway
1,9 to 23rd Street

Credit Cards
Cash Only

Cafeteria

119 7TH AVENUE @ 17TH STREET
(212) 414-1717

We don't remember cafeteria food ever looking or tasting this good. This old-school diner with a pre-millennium make over and moderately priced menu is chic Americana. The patrons in the Zen-like lounge downstairs should clue you in to the type of scene this place serves up. It's open 24 hours and it's the 'in' crowd's new hangout. Instead of milk this place serves up a mean martini. Don't forget your lunch money and don't forget to make reservations, dinner is a mad house.

Type of Establishment
Restaurant/ Lounge

Hours
Daily 24 hrs

Drink Prices
$$$

Food
American

Nearest Subway
1,2,3,9 to 14th Street

Credit Cards
All Major

Cheetah

12 WEST 21ST STREET
BETWEEN 5TH & 6TH AVENUE
(212) 206-7770

"The cheetah is the fastest
animal in the world and we
wanted this place to represent a
club in motion," said General Manager
Mitchell Stephens of this Chelsea nightclub.
Let's just hope this place never loses its spots
because it's definitely one of the hottest in
New York. As predicted, everything upstairs
is covered in the leopard's signature pattern.
The dance floor is a little on the tight side, but
you can deal. Mariah Carey swears by the
place and a number of other celebrities have
been spotted (pardon the pun) in the elevated
booths or downstairs chillin' in the lounge.

Type of Establishment
Club

Hours
Daily 10pm-4am
Closed Wed.

Drink Prices
$$$$

Food
N/A

Nearest Subway
N,R to 23rd St

Credit Cards
All Major

$20 Cover

Ciel Rouge

176 7TH AVENUE
BETWEEN 20TH & 21ST STREET
(212) 929-5542

Pre-Perestroika Moscow or Old Havana?
The compañeros running this cocktail lounge
seem to keep a secret under the red sky,
where everything, from the velvet curtain to
the tablecloth (with cigarette burns) and the
waiter's jacket, is red. Enigmatic wall and
ceiling paintings, ancient versions of *La
Bamba* and R&B imply nostalgia from
another era. An eclectic, unpretentious crowd
of insiders and passers-by enjoy real, long
and smoky conversations. Listen to piano on
Tuesdays and accordion on Thursdays while
slurping the famous Caipirinhas, and if
you're lucky, they'll open the cozy garden.

Type of Establishment
Lounge

Hours
Su-Th 7pm-2am
F-Sa 7pm-4am

Drink Prices
$$$

Food
N/A

Nearest Subway
1,9 to
23rd Street

Credit Cards
Cash Only

Downtime

251 WEST 30TH STREET
BETWEEN 7TH & 8TH AVENUE
(212) 695-2747

If you ask a manager what type of music is
played at Downtime he will answer simply
and accurately "everything." The festive
murals that depict a variety of musical scenes
are as eclectic as the mix of up-and-coming
bands that play everything from rock to reg-
gae. Everyone's ensured a great view of the
band even if you're sitting at the bar. The live
music venue has transformed its mezzanine
into a lounge and the upstairs has a game
room (check out the *X-Files* pinball machine)
and a dance floor filled with eardrum-crush-
ing speakers.

Type of Establishment
Bar/Live Music

Hours
M-Th 5pm-2am
F-Sa 5pm-4am
Su 7pm-4am

Drink Prices
$$

Food
N/A

Nearest Subway
1,9 to
28th Street

Credit Cards
All Major

Dusk

147 WEST 24TH STREET
BETWEEN 6TH & 7TH AVENUE
(212) 924-4490

Slightly off the beaten path, Dusk is a laid-back neighborhood Chelsea lounge more than anything else. You'll find a mixed crowd, though leaning towards more gay than straight on some nights. Remodeled annually, this year's version is a Miami art deco approach done in a deep shade of blue complemented by an entire wall of cut glass. The layout at Dusk is long and sleek and with plenty of lounge sofas to fall into. DJs most nights spin the right songs to complete that essential laid-back lounge atmosphere. Note: Check out the red-light bathrooms with one-way glass looking out into the bar area.

Type of Establishment
Lounge

Hours
M-W 6pm-2am
Th-Sa 6pm-4am

Drink Prices
$$$

Food
N/A

Nearest Subway
1,9 to
23rd Street

Credit Cards
All Major

East of 8th

254 WEST 23RD STREET
BETWEEN 7TH & 8TH AVENUE
(212) 352-0075

When the trendier places have overstayed their welcome and people tire of battling bitchy doormen, East of 8th will be here waiting for all of you prodigal children to come home. The menu for this gay friendly bar/restaurant is largely American fare, but the chef has been known to throw in an occasional twist. It's a shame that the only view the bay windows offer are of a Krispy Kreme doughnut shop, but the stunning open-air garden downstairs, complete with palm trees, a mini-fountain and a pond filled with goldfish, is perfect for a midsummer night's dream.

Type of Establishment
Bar/Restaurant

Hours
Daily 12pm-4am

Drink Prices
$$

Food
Eclectic American

Nearest Subway
C,E,1,9 to
23rd Street

Credit Cards
All Major

El Flamingo

547 WEST 21ST STREET
BETWEEN 10TH & 11TH AVENUE
(212) 243-2121

Saturday nights at El Flamingo are muy, muy caliente. Leave the Macarena at home with your grandmother. Here, suave hombres and sexy mujeres get down and dirty to the infectious music played by live salsa, meringue and Latin jazz bands. After a night full of spins and dips you will leave here drenched and screaming, "Olé!" If you have two left feet or are unfamiliar with the patented roll of the hips and the quick shuffle steps don't fret, dance lessons are offered from 4-6 p.m. for $10 and you get free admission for the night.

Type of Establishment
Club

Hours
Th-F 6pm-4am
Sa 10pm-5am
Su 6pm-2am

Drink Prices
$$$

Food
N/A

Nearest Subway
C,E to
23rd Street

Credit Cards
MC,V

Flowers
21 WEST 17TH STREET
BETWEEN 5TH & 6TH AVENUE
(212) 691-8888

Roses, tulips, lilies you name it — flowers are in full bloom at this Chelsea restaurant. Some of the floral arrangements are a little gauche, but this split-level still has a nice French provincial feel to it, particularly the dining room modeled after a barn with beautiful stained glass fixtures. The food is American with Mediterranean influences. If you grow weary of the women in cardigans dutifully wrapped around their shoulders and men in perfectly ironed J. Crew khakis, head upstairs to the garden and catch your breath.

Type of Establishment
Bar/Restaurant

Hours
Daily 12pm-1am

Drink Prices
$$$$

Food
American/
Mediterranean

Nearest Subway
F,L to 14th Street

Credit Cards
All Major

Fred's Beauty Bar
4 WEST 22ND STREET
BETWEEN 5TH & 6TH AVENUE
(212) 463-0888

The beauty in this bar, named after a discontinued Cuban cigar from the 20s, is found in the glass blown chandeliers resembling a festive bouquet of colorful balloons. Manager/Chef Sui Lon Chon and her amicable staff are an absolute delight. They fill this gigantic loft space with a whole lot of warmth and great energy. The mezzanine overlooking the main floor seats 50 comfortably and houses an antique shoe shine stand that is open for business. Coming from its newly renovated kitchen is an eclectic menu with Persian, African and Asian influences.

Type of Establishment
Bar/Restaurant

Hours
M-F 5pm-4am
Sa-Su 7pm-4am

Drink Prices
$$$

Food
Persian/Asian

Nearest Subway
N,R to
23rd Street

Credit Cards
All Major

G Lounge
223 WEST 19TH STREET
BETWEEN 7TH & 8TH AVENUE
(212) 929-1085

"G" as in …Gorgeous …Gregarious …Gay? A hundred pairs of eyes belonging to savagely tanned, gym-chiseled, protein-shake physiques scrutinize every body that enters this coolly designed after-work locale of gay professionals in designer t-shirts. You can mingle and check out the scene around the bustling circular bar, relax in the lounge area with a frozen Cosmopolitan, or sip an espresso in the back. Tolerable disco decibels, dim lights and a solid happy hour make this a popular meeting spot before hitting the clubs. "In gay bars, the attention is usually on a TV, here it's on people," said a 23-year-old playwright who had just been stood up.

Type of Establishment
Bar/Lounge

Hours
Daily 4pm-4am

Drink Prices
$$

Food
N/A

Nearest Subway
1,9 to
18th Street

Credit Cards
MC,V

Type of Establishment
Live Music

Hours
Varies Daily

Drink Prices
$$$

Food
N/A

Nearest Subway
A,C,E to 34th Street

Credit Cards
All Major
Tickets only

Hammerstein Ballroom
311 WEST 34TH STREET
BETWEEN 8TH & 9TH AVENUE
(212) 564-4882

The historic Manhattan Opera House, first built by Oscar Hammerstein at the turn of the century, has been turned into the multi-functional Hammerstein Ballroom featuring everything from concerts to fashion shows and industry parties. Hammerstein designed all of his theaters himself with a focus on acoustics, offering sound quality rare among halls this size. The Ballroom includes over 20,000 square feet of space with two balconies and a stage. A recent face lift puts the Hammerstein at the head of the pack at a time when many large-scale NYC venues are in desperate need of a make over.

Type of Establishment
Bar/Restaurant

Hours
Daily 5:30pm-2am

Drink Prices
$$$$

Food
Southern

Nearest Subway
1,9,F to 23rd Street

Credit Cards
MC,V,AmEx

Justin's
31 WEST 21ST STREET
BETWEEN 5TH & 6TH AVENUE
(212) 352-0599

Rap mogul Sean "Puff Daddy" Combs already has the record industry on lock down. So what does he decide to do next? Open a soul food restaurant in Chelsea. The bistro hosts New York's finest bes and wannabes. Puffy's labelmates, athletes, models and movie stars can all be found in the high-backed booths feasting on smothered chicken, collard greens and macaroni. If you're not in the mood for dinner, hang out up front at the bar. It can be a bit of a meat market, but a relatively harmless one.

Type of Establishment
Bar/Restaurant

Hours
Daily 4pm-4am

Drink Prices
$$$

Food
French

Nearest Subway
C,E,1,9 to 23rd Street

Credit Cards
All Major

La Maison de Sade
206 WEST 23RD STREET
BETWEEN 7TH & 8TH AVENUE
(212) 727-8642

The podium, shaped like a red leather rib-crushing corset, is only a hint of what you'll find in this painfully pleasurable S&M restaurant. La Maison de Sade serves up French cuisine, but who can concentrate on food when a vampish dominatrix in knee-high boots, fishnet stockings and a leather teddy screams, "harder, harder, hurt me baby …" Don't bring your Bible study group here and don't leave without purchasing a souvenir leather paddle. What's that old saying? No pain, no gain.

Lola

30 WEST 22ND STREET
BETWEEN 5TH & 6TH AVENUE
(212) 675-6700

Lying on a plush bed of black beans, wearing a headdress made of crisp plantains, Lola invites you to dive in and devour. But like a fine wine that's been sitting for decades, you must savor her slowly. Take your time, soak up the jovial energy of the dining room, and tap your feet to the infectious beats cranking from the R&B funk band in the front room. The psychic, reading palms and tarot cards ($25), predicted your future as soon as you walked in. "You will fall in love with Lola and her famous fried chicken."

Type of Establishment
Bar/Restaurant

Hours
T-Sa 6pm-
11:30pm

Drink Prices
$$$

Food
Eclectic
American

Nearest Subway
N,R to
23rd Street

Credit Cards
All Major

Lot 61

550 WEST 21ST STREET
BETWEEN 10TH & 11TH AVENUE
(212) 243-6555

Though Lot 61 came from humble beginnings (it used to be a truck stop), like most of its patrons it has moved up in the world. Dressed in everything *Vogue* said was worth buying this season, old Upper East Side money and downtown nouveau riche mingle over smoked salmon wraps and tuna summer rolls. The usual suspects have dubbed this one of 'the' places to be ... at least for the time being. But if you're not a part of the glitterati or can't do a good impersonation, don't bother coming — you might feel like a fat girl at home on prom night.

Type of Establishment
Bar/Lounge

Hours
M-Th 6pm-2am
F-Sa 6pm-3am

Drink Prices
$$$$

Food
American Tapas

Nearest Subway
C,E to
23rd Street

Credit Cards
All Major

Merchants NY

112 7TH AVENUE @ 17TH STREET
(212) 366-7267

Residents and corporate-types come for the famous martinis (try the dirty martini with pepper and olive juice), eclectic wines after work, and dinner at the outdoor cafe on busy Seventh Avenue or the mezzanine overlooking the bar, while others get a little closer downstairs on hand-made sofas near the fireplace. Ibrahim Merchant, who also owns two Merchants uptown, has the Eastern sense for making stressed-out Westerners (especially women) relax. Warm colors, soothing mandala pictures, attentive service all in a sophisticated, stylish yet romantic and unpretentious setting. It gets packed after 5:30 p.m. and there are lines on the weekend.

Type of Establishment
Bar/Restaurant/
Lounge

Hours
Daily 11:30am-
4am

Drink Prices
$$$

Food
American

Nearest Subway
1,9 to
18th Street

Credit Cards
All Major

Mimosa

215 WEST 28TH STREET
BETWEEN 7TH & 8TH AVENUE
(212) 643-1199

DJs spin and live entertainers perform salsa,
meringue, house and R&B for a packed
crowd most Friday and Saturday nights,
bringing a Latin flavor to Chelsea on the
weekends. This spot features two floors
with music and lights, a fully stocked bar,
two hi-tech DJ booths, four TV monitors
and a professional light show. A restaurant
by day, the tables are taken out and the
entire first floor becomes a dance floor.

Type of Establishment
Bar

Hours
Th-Sa 10pm-4am

Drink Prices
$$

Food
N/A

Nearest Subway
1,9 to
28th Street

Credit Cards
Cash Only

Mother

432 WEST 14TH STREET @ WASHINGTON
(212) 366-5680

There's no better place to have a coming out
party than here at Mother ... and we're not
talking about an old-fashioned cotillion.
Most of the regular soirées held here are very
gay friendly, particularly Clit Club, the Friday
night lesbian party that's been around for
eight years. The Click-n-Drag party (how
clever) on Saturday nights mixes a spoonful
of technology, with a smidgen of rubber and
a cup of leather. You know, all those fetishes
that make the world go 'round.

Type of Establishment
Club

Hours
T-Su 10pm-5am

Drink Prices
$$$$

Food
N/A

Nearest Subway
A,C,E to
14th Street

Credit Cards
MC,V,AmEx

Ohm

16 WEST 22ND STREET
BETWEEN 5TH & 6TH AVENUE
(212) 229-2000

Is this amalgam of high-tech spaceship,
Roman coliseum and shopping mall the
ultimate club experience? Droning house
and techno music resounds in the sleek,
unadorned galaxy divided by oversized cur-
tains, where a relentless party crowd of
twenty-something professionals in black min-
gles with drinks in their hands at the front
bar and the elevated lounge area, dines in
endlessly long, fabric-upholstered couches at
the gallery restaurant, and dances itself into
illumination on the expansive dance floor in
front of a coolly lit, glass-tiled heaven's gate
that must lead to Ohm (or was it Nirvana?)

Type of Establishment
Club

Hours
W 5pm-3am
Th-Sa 5pm-4am
Su 9pm-4am

Drink Prices
$$$

Food
Creole

Nearest Subway
N,R,F to
23rd Street

Credit Cards
MC,V,AmEx

Opera

539 WEST 21ST STREET
BETWEEN 10TH & 11TH AVENUE
(212) 229-1618

Did they have basketball players, leggy super-models or jolly green giants in mind when they furnished this place? The custom-made couches are not only exquisite one-of-a-kinds, but they're colossal and comfortable. Reminiscent of furniture from *Alice in Wonderland* you can't help but feel like a Lilliputian when you sit in the cheetah-skin covered throne. The only things small here are the gym bunnies in tight black minis and even tighter black blouses that serve up rather expensive cocktails. But Opera attracts an older more upscale crowd, the type of crowd that can afford to pay $10-$15 for a drink.

Type of Establishment
Club

Hours
W-Sa 11pm-4am

Drink Prices
$$$$

Food
N/A

Nearest Subway
C,E to
23rd Street

Credit Cards
MC,V,AmEx

Rebar

127 8TH AVENUE @ 16TH STREET
(212) 627-1680

If you're looking for the hippest spot in town, Rebar is not it. The crowd doesn't sparkle, there's no real scene, just a roomful of everyday people dancing to good music. But what's wrong with that, does every place in New York have to be stellar? No. The only cool thing in Rebar is the floor made out of beautiful mosaic tiles, but again, who needs cool when they're groovin'. No attitude, no delusions of grandeur, just a fun-loving and unpretentious good time.

Type of Establishment
Bar/Lounge

Hours
T-Sa 8pm-4am

Drink Prices
$$$

Food
N/A

Nearest Subway
A,C,E to
14th Street

Credit Cards
MC,V,AmEx

Roxy

515 WEST 18TH STREET
BETWEEN 10TH & 11TH STREET
(212) 645-5156

When you grow tired of New York's ubiquitous lounge scene, head over to the legendary Roxy — it's one of the few clubs left standing from the 80s. With a huge dance floor (the largest in the city), strobe lights and disco balls, Saturday night is gay, gay, gay. "Actually it's about the largest gay nightclub in the city and probably the largest in the country," said owner Gene Dinineo. Voguing to the house beats of DJ Victor Calderone (he does Madonna's mixes), drag queens abound (approximately 2,000 strong) but everyone's welcome and everyone comes. So just shut up and dance.

Type of Establishment
Club

Hours
F-Sa 11pm-7am

Drink Prices
$$$

Food
N/A

Nearest Subway
A,C,E to
14th Street

Credit Cards
Cash Only

$20 Cover

Splash

50 WEST 17TH STREET
BETWEEN 5TH & 6TH AVENUE
(212) 691-0073

For anybody sick of Chelsea's attitude, head down to Splash, a more friendly, relaxed and not-as-dressed-up gay club. Refreshingly, they are female friendly too, and plenty of women appear to favor it as a result. The dance floor is packed on Saturday night, so you can flee to the pool room or to the bar downstairs. More international and touristy than some of the gay bars in Chelsea. The drinks are cheap, the music good (anything from disco to 80s to current dance), and the almost-naked male go-go dancers provide live entertainment.

Type of Establishment
Club/Lounge

Hours
Daily 4pm-4am

Drink Prices
$$

Food
N/A

Nearest Subway
1,2,3,9 to 14th Street

Credit Cards
Cash Only

Tramps

51 WEST 21ST STREET
BETWEEN 5TH & 6TH AVENUE
(212) 727-7788

One of the few music dives in New York that remains as unassuming and genuine as a small town music festival. Enjoy yourself just the way you are, in 80s jeans and sneakers, cowboy hat or hippie garb, to live Cajun, country, funk, jazz and swing bands. Single women will politely be asked to dance, and a generous, undivided space allows those who found each other to do so from the stage all the way to the beautiful, classy wood bar whose cast iron railing reminisces of old Western movies, swirling past loosely set tables where some may stop for fine Cajun food and a beer.

Type of Establishment
Bar/Live Music

Hours
Daily 12pm-4am

Drink Prices
$$

Food
Cajun

Nearest Subway
N,R,F to 23rd Street

Credit Cards
MC,V,AmEx

GRAMERCY

© ANDRE JUNGET '98

No longer identified as the polarized stage of one distinct socioeconomic or political faction, Gramercy has reinvented itself as the crossroads of New York City.

Originally where the Roosevelts and Astors built their mansions, Gramercy was once considered the epicenter of old New York high society. That time has long passed. The magnates and tycoons were eventually replaced by political radicals and experimental artists. It became home to the Communist Party headquarters for a while and later Andy Warhol's infamous Factory. During the 70s, like many downtown neighborhoods, Gramercy fell victim to a drug-fueled decline. The playground of upper-crust society at one time, the battleground for political and artistic radicalism at another, Gramercy has come a long way and reemerged with a new identity.

In the sidewalk cafes, swanky bars and upscale restaurants, downtown meets uptown as in no other neighborhood in the city. At the center of this cultural commotion is Union Square. Stand on the corner of 16th Street and Park Avenue South and cast your eyes uptown. Then cross through the park and stand on Broadway and 14th Street and look downtown. Two sharply contrasting viewpoints of two separate worlds, yet just a few feet from each other and both draining into Gramercy. This sea of excitement and emotion has produced one of the most unique and enjoyable nightlife experiences in the city.

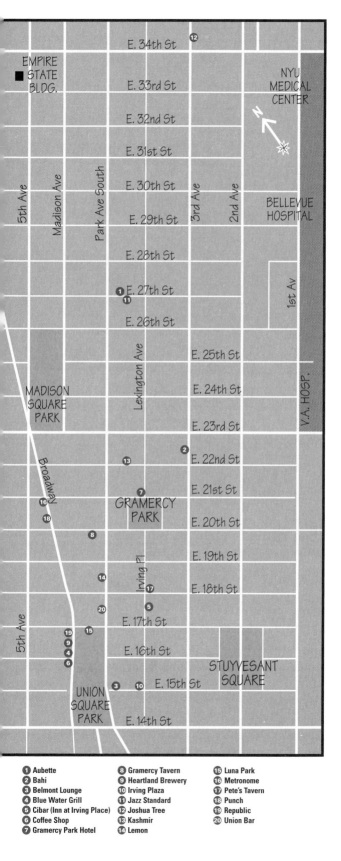

E. 34th St ⑫

EMPIRE STATE BLDG. ■

E. 33rd St

E. 32nd St

E. 31st St

E. 30th St

E. 29th St

E. 28th St

① E. 27th St
⑪

E. 26th St

E. 25th St

E. 24th St

E. 23rd St

② E. 22nd St
⑬

⑦ E. 21st St

GRAMERCY PARK E. 20th St

⑯ E. 19th St
⑱

⑧

⑭ E. 18th St
⑰

⑳
E. 17th St
⑲ ⑤
⑨
⑮ E. 16th St
④
⑥

③ ⑩ E. 15th St

UNION SQUARE PARK

E. 14th St

5th Ave
Madison Ave
Park Ave South
Lexington Ave
3rd Ave
2nd Ave
1st Av
Broadway
Irving Pl
5th Ave

NYU MEDICAL CENTER

BELLEVUE HOSPITAL

V.A. HOSP.

MADISON SQUARE PARK

STUYVESANT SQUARE

N

① Aubette
② Bahi
③ Belmont Lounge
④ Blue Water Grill
⑤ Cibar (Inn at Irving Place)
⑥ Coffee Shop
⑦ Gramercy Park Hotel

⑧ Gramercy Tavern
⑨ Heartland Brewery
⑩ Irving Plaza
⑪ Jazz Standard
⑫ Joshua Tree
⑬ Kashmir
⑭ Lemon

⑮ Luna Park
⑯ Metronome
⑰ Pete's Tavern
⑱ Punch
⑲ Republic
⑳ Union Bar

Aubette

119 EAST 27TH STREET
BETWEEN PARK & LEXINGTON
(212) 686-5500

Aubette stands out in the otherwise lackluster neighborhood of Kips Bay, and it's not just because of the decor. Evoking an 'industrial meets 50s modernist' aesthetic, with its leather couches, silver metal chairs and tables, functioning fireplace and cozy cigar room in the back, Aubette is worth a visit for visual appeal alone. With its food menu available till closing, 22 different wines by the glass, 37 single malt scotch varieties, 11 different champagnes — Aubette is perfect date material. But if you're looking for a night out with the boys (or girls), stay away. Dress suitably — i.e., New York chic.

Type of Establishment
Bar/Restaurant

Hours
M-F 5pm-4am
Sa-Su 7pm-4am

Drink Prices
$$$

Food
Eclectic

Nearest Subway
6 to 28th Street

Credit Cards
All Major

Bahi

284 3RD AVENUE
BETWEEN 22ND & 23RD STREET
(212) 254-5466

Capitalizing on the current craze for all things spiritual, Bahi, the new kid on the traditionally Irish pub block, is a trendy bar with a whole lot of 'South Asian meets MTV' attitude. The bar's name means karma, fate, destiny — you know those words that self-help gurus like Deepak Chopra love to say while inhaling and exhaling ever so slowly. After enjoying a few drinks in the front room, head to the ashrams hidden deep in the back. Sink into a leather bean bag, cross your legs, close your eyes and connect with your inner child.

Type of Establishment
Bar/Lounge

Hours
Daily 5pm-4am

Drink Prices
$$

Food
N/A

Nearest Subway
6 to 23rd Street

Credit Cards
All Major

Belmont Lounge

117 EAST 15TH STREET
BETWEEN IRVING PLACE &
UNION SQUARE EAST
(212) 533-0009

What do you say about a place where Mariah Carey has her birthday party? Or when Robert De Niro and Helena Christensen pop in? Belmont Lounge is très cool — with its dimly lit booths at the back, separated by thin curtains, or its outdoor seating area — people flock here like crazy. A lot of NYU students hang here, but you'll also spot the occasional celebrity and other glamorous and wannabe glams cruising the shabby chic surroundings. Every other month they feature a different artist on the walls, so if you want art and music in a hip and cool surrounding, come on down.

Type of Establishment
Restaurant/ Lounge

Hours
Daily 4pm-4am

Drink Prices
$$

Food
American

Nearest Subway
4,5,6,N,R to Union Sq

Credit Cards
All Major

Blue Water Grill

31 UNION SQUARE WEST @ 16TH STREET
(212) 675-9500

Indulge in the grandiose
ambiance of this 100-year-
old New York landmark
with marble walls and
stucco ceilings as lofty and
beautiful as the sky. An upscale but unpretentious mixed crowd gathers here after
work for a drink or dinner, turning the place
into a bustling, high-energy spot. The huge
space is smartly divided into a central bar,
several dining areas, a raw bar, and, best of
all, an elevated terrace that allows you to
watch Union Square's uptown-meets-down-
town scene. A hip, up-tempo mood prevails
in the downstairs dining room featuring a
small cigar bar and live jazz six nights a week.

Type of Establishment
Bar/Restaurant

Hours
M-Th 11:30am-
    12:30am
F-Sa 11:30am-
    1am

Drink Prices
$$$

Food
Seafood

Nearest Subway
4,5,6,N,R to
Union Sq

Credit Cards
MC,V,AmEx

Cibar (Inn at Irving Place)

56 IRVING PLACE
BETWEEN 17TH & 18TH STREET
(212) 460-5656

One of many cigar bars cropping up all over
the city, Cibar has the advantage of its lovely
locale: idyllic Irving Place and its cozy inte-
rior. Unlike most other cigar bars, this one
actually looks, and is, female friendly.
Whether it's the upholstered couches or the
intimate feel, a lot of women seem to agree:
the crowd on any given night is evenly split
across gender lines. Choose from an exten-
sive list of single malt scotches and martinis,
stroll out to the small outdoor space (front
and back), and enjoy the evening. The feel?
Upper East Side bankers venture downtown.

Type of Establishment
Bar

Hours
M-Th 5pm-2am
F-Sa 5pm-4am

Drink Prices
$$$$

Food
N/A

Nearest Subway
4,5,6,N,R to
Union Sq

Credit Cards
MC,V,AmEx

Coffee Shop

29 UNION SQUARE WEST @ 16TH STREET
(212) 243-7969

Don't let its classic American diner look fool
you, there's nothing down home about this
celebrity hangout. Notorious for hiring only
those who look like they've sauntered down
a catwalk in Paris, it's painfully obvious that
if you don't look mahvelous darling, you
need not apply. Long-legged vixens and well-
sculpted studs serve up Brazilian cuisine
(entrees $10-$15). The juice bar features
exotic health drinks that promise to make
you strong and sexy, but wouldn't you rather
be stuffing yourself silly with the Shop's
famous banana cream pie?

Type of Establishment
Bar/Restaurant

Hours
Su-M 7am-2am
T-Sa 7am-6am

Drink Prices
$$$

Food
American/
Brazilian

Nearest Subway
4,5,6,N,R to
Union Sq

Credit Cards
MC,V,AmEx

Type of
Establishment
Bar/Restaurant

Hours
Daily 10am-
12am

Drink Prices
$$

Food
American

Nearest
Subway
6 to 23rd Street

Credit Cards
All Major

Gramercy Park Hotel
2 LEXINGTON AVENUE @ 21ST STREET
(212) 475-4320

This warm, old-world bar is a 'must see' for anyone in New York. First of all, it's in a great location in that cozy and beautiful square called Gramercy Park. Second, it's the perfect place for a tête-à-tête with a date, friend, colleague, etc. Third, the drinks are good, which shouldn't be taken for granted in New York. Although you may not normally think to go to a hotel bar, this one is worth the visit.

Type of
Establishment
Bar/Restaurant

Hours
Su-Th 12pm-
11pm
F-Sa 12pm-12am

Drink Prices
$$$

Food
Fine American

Nearest
Subway
4,5,6,N,R to
Union Sq

Credit Cards
MC,V,AmEx

Gramercy Tavern
42 EAST 20TH STREET
BETWEEN BROADWAY & PARK AVENUE SOUTH
(212) 477-0777

The bar at Gramercy Tavern is perfect for cocktailing. Swanky and upscale (both the space and the crowd), the bar features an older, suit and jacket set. On the weekends, it still favors an older crowd, but instead of suits, you'll find blazers and shorter skirts. A very good date bar or even a good place to meet up as a very small group. Drinks are on the pricier side, but that's in keeping with the upscale ambiance, and you can actually converse without shouting.

Type of
Establishment
Bar/Restaurant

Hours
M-Th 12pm-1am
F-Sa 12pm-2am
Su 12pm-12am

Drink Prices
$$$

Food
American

Nearest
Subway
4,5,6,N,R to
Union Sq

Credit Cards
All Major

Heartland Brewery
35 UNION SQUARE WEST
BETWEEN 16TH & 17TH STREET
(212) 645-3400

Heartland Brewery has the rare combination of a friendly atmosphere, attentive wait staff, and great food and drink. Even non-beer drinkers will enjoy their homemade brew — a tasting menu offers the best value for the money. All the beers are delicious, and they make a mean buffalo burger. The space is long, with full seating upstairs and downstairs (it gets crowded quickly in the evenings, so call in advance for a table). A 1997 gold medal winner at the Great American Beer Festival, it's no wonder this is the oldest microbrewery in the City, with a recently opened second branch in midtown.

Irving Plaza
17 IRVING PLACE @ 15TH STREET
(212) 777-6800

A music Mecca like New York City deserves a venue like Irving Plaza. Dwarfed in comparison to the larger Roseland and Hammerstein Ballrooms of the Manhattan concert landscape, it is actually its size that is its best attribute. Whether swaying to Jewel or slamming to the Beastie Boys, Irving Plaza's exceptional acoustics allow you to sense every chord and swallow every syllable. Test your skills at intense crowd cohabitation, but make sure to leave the white shoes at home and expect to sweat. Note: Tickets for certain shows sell out quickly, so lineup early.

Type of Establishment
Live Music

Hours
Varies Daily

Drink Prices
$$

Food
N/A

Nearest Subway
4,5,6,N,R to Union Sq

Credit Cards
MC,V,AmEx
Tickets Only

Jazz Standard
116 EAST 27TH STREET
BETWEEN PARK AVENUE SOUTH &
LEXINGTON
(212) 576-2232

Across the street from Aubette, upstairs at 27 Standard is a restaurant and bar area, downstairs is the jazz club. Come here for the downstairs — the jazz club is large, with two separate sections for smoking and non, a bar area with table service and a complete menu to choose from. The cover is $10 (sometimes $15) and is well worth it. The upstairs bar area is stuffy and has a transitory feel to it — as though people are just waiting by the bar pondering their next step. Take our suggestion and make a beeline for downstairs.

Type of Establishment
Jazz Club

Hours
T-Th 9, 10:30pm
F-Sa 8, 10:30pm,
12am
Su 7pm

Drink Prices
$$$

Food
Contemporary American

Nearest Subway
6 to 28th Street

Credit Cards
All Major

$15 Cover
+ $10 Food/Drink
Minimum

Joshua Tree
513 3RD AVENUE
BETWEEN 34TH & 35TH STREET
(212) 689-0058

Ever since this sports bar-cum-restaurant opened, it's been packed every night of the week. Located in the heart of Murray Hill, Joshua Tree has cashed in on the local twenty-something singles scene in the area. The drinks are well priced, the food is so-so but the space is big, and the three together make for a winning combination. Not recommended for a weekend night unless you want to jockey for space or cruise for the opposite sex. Best on a weeknight and best if you're from the neighborhood.

Type of Establishment
Bar/Restaurant

Hours
Daily 11am-4am

Drink Prices
$$

Food
American

Nearest Subway
6 to 33rd Street

Credit Cards
All Major

Type of Establishment
Bar/Lounge

Hours
M-Sa 6pm-3am

Drink Prices
$$$$

Food
N/A

Nearest Subway
6 to 23rd Street

Credit Cards
All Major

Kashmir

111 EAST 22ND STREET
BETWEEN PARK AVENUE SOUTH &
LEXINGTON
(212) 460-5867

With wall-to-wall carpeting, a curvy blue velvet couch and a surround-sound stereo system, Kashmir definitely looks like a hip bachelor pad plucked from the pages of *Metropolitan Home*. The tiger print bar stools are a godsend. They have extra padding for back support, more than enough room for any size derrière, and are by far the most comfortable in the city. Like the steady stream of models that regularly pour into the place — Elite modeling agency is next door — this place knows how to work it.

Type of Establishment
Bar/Restaurant/
Lounge

Hours
Daily 11:30am-
4am

Drink Prices
$$$

Food
American/Thai

Nearest Subway
4,5,6,N,R to
Union Sq

Credit Cards
MC,V,AmEx

Lemon

230 PARK AVENUE SOUTH
BETWEEN 18TH & 19TH STREET
(212) 614-1200

One of the luminaries of a rejuvenated downtown Park Avenue, Lemon has a loyal following, lots of tourists and private parties that ensure its success. The hotel lobbyish feel extends to the cafe area where tables and chairs face out toward the bustling avenue — ideal for those who enjoy people watching. High ceiling fans and waiters in Nehru jackets also lend to the vibe. The upstairs, loungey with its plush green couches, is more intimate and cozy and depending on the time of day, quieter. Make reservations if you want a table.

Type of Establishment
Bar/Restaurant

Hours
May-October
Daily 12pm-
12am

Drink Prices
$$

Food
Mediterranean

Nearest Subway
4,5,6,N,R to
Union Sq

Credit Cards
MC,V,AmEx

Luna Park

50 EAST 17TH STREET
@ UNION SQUARE PARK
(212) 475-8464

The disclaimer "weather permitting" is a phrase any place with no roof must get used to. Mother Nature pulls the strings at this outdoor Mediterranean-style restaurant. The semi-circular space resembles an open-air amphitheater. Fold up chairs, plastic white tables, and huge umbrellas lend to the patio party feel of the seasonal restaurant (only open from May to October). It's a great place to soak up the sun, sip on some bubbly, and escape from all the hustle and bustle madness of Union Square.

Metronome

915 Broadway @ 21st Street
(212) 505-7400

Despite the ridiculous indoor VIP velvet rope
that's supposed to cordon off the chosen few
from the rest of us regular folk, pseudo-
industry types still mingle with the shot
callers on the dance floor. Designer labels
abound and being understated is not an
option. The mezzanine lounge is perfect for
profiling, and judging from the number of
people on their cell phones or checking their
pagers, apparently you must at least look
busy while sitting in one of the booths.

Type of Establishment
Bar/Restaurant/Club

Hours
T-Th 5pm-12am
F-Sa 5pm-4am

Drink Prices
$$$

Food
Mediterranean

Nearest Subway
N,R to 23rd Street

Credit Cards
MC,V,AmEx

Pete's Tavern

129 East 18th Street @ Irving Place
(212) 473-7676

Opened in 1864, Pete's is the oldest continu-
ally operating establishment in the city. The
front room of the pub still has its original tin
ceiling, tile floor, antique mirrors and rose-
wood bar. It's the type of place that prompts
crotchety old men to say, "They don't make
places like they used to." Visit the shrine
above booth #3 and you'll understand why
the pub is nicknamed "The place O. Henry
made famous." Epic proportions of Italian
and American cuisine are served at this bar
with three cozy dining rooms. Leave your
belts at home, we promise, behemoth ham-
burgers are just the beginning.

Type of Establishment
Bar/Restaurant

Hours
Daily 11am-2am

Drink Prices
$$

Food
Italian/American

Nearest Subway
4,5,6,N,R to Union Sq

Credit Cards
All Major

Punch

913 Broadway
Between 20th & 21st Street
(212) 673-6333

There is something refreshingly light and
southern going on in this bar/restaurant.
The intimate bar and bistro scene is domi-
nated by an interesting mix of young artists,
fashion designers, Europeans and aging hip-
pies. Girlfriends seem to love meeting here,
quietly chatting away against world music.
Following the floor mosaic, steal a juicy
olive from the big plate at the bar, and wind
up in the chic restaurant with its inspira-
tional transparent and gold organza curtains
and fabric-covered chairs. Join the suits and
fashion pros as they feast on an intricate
mix of eclectic American dishes.

Type of Establishment
Bar/Restaurant

Hours
Daily 12pm-1am

Drink Prices
$$$

Food
Eclectic American

Nearest Subway
4,5,6,N,R to Union Sq

Credit Cards
All Major

Republic

37 UNION SQUARE WEST
BETWEEN 16TH & 17TH STREET
(212) 627-7172

Type of Establishment
Bar/Restaurant

Hours
Su-W 12pm-11pm
Th-Sa 12pm-12am

Drink Prices
$$$

Food
Pan-Asian

Nearest Subway
4,5,6,N,R to Union Sq

Credit Cards
All Major

Uptown sophisticated, yet with a downtown casual accent, Republic is the definitive chic upscale eatery and bar. Enjoy an outdoor table overlooking Union Square or venture inside and grab a seat at one of the communal style tables that encourages rapport. A delicious menu of French-Vietnamese and Thai cuisine keeps them coming back, as does the exceptional symmetrical architecture that gives you the impression you are visiting an art gallery instead of a public house.

Union Bar

204 PARK AVENUE SOUTH
BETWEEN 17TH & 18TH STREET
(212) 674-2105

Type of Establishment
Bar

Hours
Daily 5pm-3am

Drink Prices
$$$

Food
Pizza

Nearest Subway
4,5,6,N,R to Union Sq

Credit Cards
MC,V,AmEx

There is a stylish interaction between jazzy coolness and wooden warmth going on behind Venetian blinds at this upscale Park Avenue South bar. The centerpiece here is obviously the voluptuously curved-wood bar, at which a sophisticated, neat corporate crowd eyes their opposite, thanks to an intricate hi-tech lighting system. All this is set against a backdrop of unadorned brown, beige and gray walls, and a mix of jazz and funk. If people watching at the bar tires you out, you may want to sink into the leather couches and chairs at the diner-like divisions behind the bar.

GREENWICH VILLAGE

© ANDRE JUNGET·98

Few other neighborhoods in the world have embedded themselves as deeply in our collective conscious as Greenwich Village.

Its winding streets have served as both sanctuary and battleground for generations of political radicals, fiery writers and starving artists. Their prose and performances have ignited great change and upheaval in the city and beyond. Just as important, though, is the neighborhood's tenacity for preserving a forum for personal and artistic expression. Many critics argue the Village has outgrown its radical mantle and abandoned its authenticity. The reality has been, however, more of a gradual maturity — sincere to the core, yet assuming the role of elder statesman over this next generation of firebrands and revolutionaries, striking out from both within and beyond its boundaries.

Thousands of visitors pour over the crooked nooks and dark crannies of Greenwich Village each day to experience and embrace the sweet independent air of unhindered artistic and lifestyle expression. R&B soulful tunes floating down Bleecker Street are assaulted in mid-air by the screeching guitar of a Kiss cover band down the block as you stroll in and out of the bars and cafes near the intersection of MacDougal. Tourists and New York University students mix with the usual suspects as you make your way through the colorfully crowded streets. Independent films, comedy, performance art, live music, 101 different rum drinks, the list goes on and on. Pay close attention and still so many things glide right by. But rest assured, whether it's a new idea, or a different way of looking at something familiar, you'll always leave with a little more than you came with.

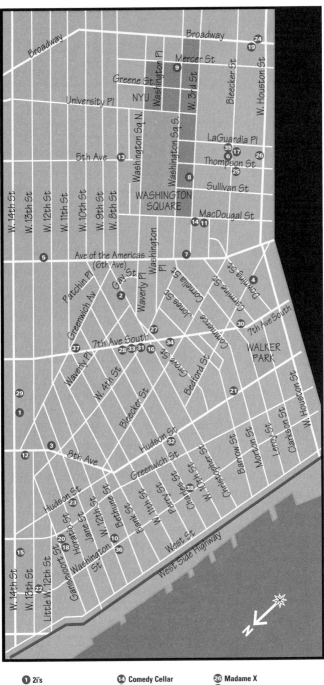

1 2i's
2 55 Bar
3 Art Bar
4 Bar D'O
5 Bar 6
6 The Bitter End
7 Blue Note
8 Boston Comedy Club
9 Bottom Line
10 Braque
11 Cafe Wha?
12 Chicago B.L.U.E.S.
13 Clementine

14 Comedy Cellar
15 The Cooler
16 Duplex Cabaret
17 The Elbow Room
18 Florent
19 Gonzalez y Gonzalez
20 Hell
21 Henrietta Hudson
22 Hogs and Heifers
23 Hudson Bar & Books
24 Louisiana Community Bar & Grill
25 Life

26 Madame X
27 The Monster
28 Moomba
29 Nell's
30 Nowbar
31 Riviera Cafe & Sports Bar
32 Ruby Fruit Bar & Grill
33 Smalls
34 Sweet Basil
35 Terra Blues
36 Tortilla Flats
37 Village Vanguard
38 Waterloo

2i's

248 WEST 14TH STREET
BETWEEN 7TH & 8TH AVENUE
(212) 807-1775

Type of Establishment
Lounge/Club

Hours
M-Sa 10pm-4am

Drink Prices
$$$

Food
N/A

Nearest Subway
1,2,3,9 to 14th Street

Credit Cards
All Major

When the joint gets jumpin' on Saturday night, which is usually after midnight, it gets hot, hot, hot. 2i's melts into a bootie-to-bootie sweat box, but the largely yuppy crowd wouldn't have it any other way. It's definitely more casual than its next door neighbor Nells, but if you came to boogie, here at 2i's you can really get jiggy wit'it. The upstairs sauna/dance floor can become unbearable, but just wipe your brow — repeatedly, head downstairs to the cool down lounge, grab a drink, and recover. There is a $10 cover, but you'll walk out of 2i's ten pounds lighter. Promise.

55 Bar

55 CHRISTOPHER STREET
BETWEEN 6TH & 7TH AVENUE SOUTH
(212) 929-9883

Type of Establishment
Bar

Hours
M-Sa 8am-4am
Su 2pm-3am

Drink Prices
$

Food
N/A

Nearest Subway
1,9 to Christopher Street

Credit Cards
Cash Only

One of the last true neighborhood bars, this former speakeasy from the 20s still lures you with the promise of something deliciously forbidden. Glide down the hidden stairs, converse with the old Bohemian couple at the upper-right-hand corner of the bar or disappear at a small table in the dark, where insider jazz aficionados, intellectuals, and a tourist or two stick their heads together. This place has no frills, but offers seven days a week what the Village used to be all about: live contemporary New York jazz and blues, an authentic alternative community feel, and, oh yes, free popcorn.

Art Bar

52 8TH AVENUE
BETWEEN JANE & HORATIO
(212) 727-0244

Type of Establishment
Bar

Hours
Daily 4pm-4am

Drink Prices
$

Food
N/A

Nearest Subway
A,C,E to 14th Street

Credit Cards
All Major

Sorry, there are no Picassos or Matisses here, and in spite of the bar's name, the art in the front room is furniture-store tacky (i.e., gold tassels hanging from mirrored canvases with indiscernible etchings). Fortunately, the ever-changing installations of original art that cover the brick walls of the lounge more than make up for the faux pas up front. The cozy little alcove, complete with fireplace, can be a little too close for comfort at times, but the neighborhood crowd of aesthetes don't appear to mind at all.

Bar D'O
29 BEDFORD STREET @ DOWNING
(212) 627-1580

The Supremes they're not, but when drag divas Sherry Vine, Sade, and Raven O get together on Saturday nights, they're fierce and infinitely entertaining. Sade beats Toni Braxton at her own game. Sherry, "like the drink," and Vine, "like the ivy," plays the dumb bombshell blonde of the group, and Raven O is the HHBIC (Hispanic head bitch in charge). Bar D'O is very gay friendly, but the cabaret also definitely attracts a huge young hetero crowd. Get there early or be prepared to catch a butt cramp sitting on the floor all night long.

Type of Establishment
Lounge

Hours
Daily 7pm-2am

Drink Prices
$$$

Food
N/A

Nearest Subway
1,9 to Houston Street

Credit Cards
Cash Only

Bar 6
502 6TH AVENUE
BETWEEN 12TH & 13TH STREET
(212) 691-1363

Though management swears the two places are not at all affiliated, and the menu on the mirrored walls and European pub-like feel of both places is just coincidence, Bar 6 does bear a striking resemblance to the French bistro Lucky Strike in SoHo. One look at the menu and its prices, however, and you'll soon discover that the places are nothing alike. Instead of French-inspired food, Bar 6's menu has Moroccan influences and instead of an average entree costing an arm AND a leg, at Bar 6 you get your choice of the two.

Type of Establishment
Bar/Restaurant

Hours
Daily 12pm-4am

Drink Prices
$$

Food
French/ Moroccan

Nearest Subway
B,D,F,Q to 14th Street

Credit Cards
All Major

The Bitter End
147 BLEECKER STREET
BETWEEN LaGUARDIA & THOMPSON
(212) 673-7030

Run by three friends who follow music to the bitter end, this 38-year-old establishment is New York's insider spot for up-and-coming bands. A long list of musicians — some of whom had their portraits painted over the bar — from Joan Baez, Miles Davis to Tori Amos, played here before and after everyone knew their name. Always packed with lively, artsy Village people who seem to know each other (and, of course, tourists), this friendly, smoky club featuring a small, intimate stage, offers alternative rock, folk, acoustic music, jazz, reggae and blues at affordable prices seven nights a week.

Type of Establishment
Bar/Live Music

Hours
Su-Th 8pm-2am
F-Sa 8pm-4am

Drink Prices
$$

Food
N/A

Nearest Subway
A,C,E,B,D,F,Q to West 4th Street

Credit Cards
All Major

Type of Establishment
Live Music

Hours
Su-Th 7pm-2am
F-Sa 7pm-4am

Drink Prices
$$$

Food
American

Nearest Subway
A,C,E,B,D,F,Q to West 4th Street

Credit Cards
All Major

Blue Note

131 WEST 3RD STREET @ 6TH AVENUE
(212) 475-8592

It's in a village, but of worldly dimensions. Tourists, as well as New York jazz aficionados, flock here and squeeze each other in to hear national headliners 365 days a year, twice nightly. The intriguing mix of the dark, cool and glamorous jazz world is reflected in the arrow-like stripes made of dark leather and mirrors, and a blue drawing of a jazz musician. Technically superb lighting and sound systems make for an impeccable jazz experience, and stars like B.B. King know how to entice the audience to snap their fingers and even sing along. CDs are available on site.

Type of Establishment
Comedy Club

Hours
Su-Th 9:30pm
F-Sa 10pm &
12:15am

Drink Prices
$$

Food
N/A

Nearest Subway
A,C,E,B,D,F,Q to West 4th Street

Credit Cards
All Major

$5-10 Cover
+ 2 Drinks

Boston Comedy Club

82 WEST 3RD STREET
BETWEEN THOMPSON & SULLIVAN
(212) 477-1000

Okay, so it's not Carolines, but up-and-coming comedians have got to have a place to work out the kinks before they have their own HBO comedy special, don't they? Monday is new talent night so you might have to sit through some "don't you hate it when…" routines, but judging from the plethora of framed head shots that cover the walls, these comedians grow out of that generic stuff and find jokes that don't require an explanation. There's nothing funny about paying an $8 cover, in addition to a two drink minimum, but at least here you can laugh it off.

Type of Establishment
Bar/Restaurant/
Live Music

Hours
Varies Nightly

Drink Prices
$$$

Food
American

Nearest Subway
A,C,E,B,D,F,Q to West 4th Street

Credit Cards
Cash Only

Bottom Line

15 WEST 4TH STREET @ MERCER
(212) 228-7880

Music lovers can't go wrong in this 24-year-old Village institution. The folk, rock, jazz and all-women acts are performed by established bands with recording contracts. The decor — wooden tables, dark pillars, bare walls and a bar in the corner — is very basic, leaving it to the musicians to illuminate this intimate space. The music styles are as eclectic as the people walking in here: nostalgic hippies, after-work crowds and punks mingle with tourists from across the ponds, especially Japanese who MUST bring back proof that they spent a night at the Bottom Line.

Braque

775 WASHINGTON STREET
@ 12TH STREET
(212) 255-0709

You've just come home from a hard day at
whatever glitzy gig you have. Rover has been
locked in the house all day and he needs some
fresh air. While walking your four-legged
friend, you're hit with an intense craving for
red wine, steak frites grilled contro filetto with
fries ($15) and some dessert. O-kay maybe
your craving isn't that specific, but you are
hungry and you know that Braque, the seasonal
open-air cafe in your West Village neighborhood, has great light fare, is the perfect place
to unwind and most importantly allows pets.

**Type of
Establishment**
Bar/Restaurant

Hours
May-October
Daily 5pm-2am

Drink Prices
$$

Food
Mediterranean

**Nearest
Subway**
A,C,E to
14th Street

Credit Cards
MC,V,AmEx

Cafe Wha?

115 MACDOUGAL STREET
BETWEEN BLEECKER & 3RD STREET
(212) 254-3706

It's Monday night and the Brazilian
songstress bellowing into the microphone is
sweating. Her band is in full swing and
they're giving the crowd all they've got (they
better; the audience did pay a $10 cover and
a two drink minimum to get in.) When it's
not the "The Brazilian B Band" whipping the
crowd into a Bacchanalian frenzy, it's "Slam
Clinic" or "The Cafe Wha? Band." Some
nights are free; others are not, but the place is
always a tight squeeze. It can get a little
stuffy, but that's never stopped the crowd
from shaking their booties.

**Type of
Establishment**
Bar/Live Music

Hours
Su-Th 8:30pm-
2:30am
F-Sa 8:30pm-
4am

Drink Prices
$$

Food
Bar Menu

**Nearest
Subway**
1,9 to
Christopher
Street

Credit Cards
MC,V,AmEx

Chicago B.L.U.E.S.

73 8TH AVENUE
BETWEEN 13TH & 14TH STREET
(212) 924-9755

Chicago B.L.U.E.S. offers the stuff good
blues is made of. Every night an assortment
of people from all over the city come here to
listen to performers like Sweet Georgia
Brown lament over lost loves, lousy friends
and all the other bittersweets that make up
why we sing the blues. Cover charge ranges
from $5-$20, but patrons don't mind paying. "It's the best blues bar in New York
because it's committed to investing in quality
performers," said a CB regular. Know what
that's called? BLUES POWER!

**Type of
Establishment**
Blues Club

Hours
Su-W 9pm,
10:30pm,
12am
Th-Sa 9:30pm,
11pm,
12:30am

Drink Prices
$$

Food
N/A

**Nearest
Subway**
A,C,E to
14th Street

Credit Cards
All Major

$5-10 Cover
+ 2 Drinks
No Cover Su-T

Type of Establishment
Bar/Restaurant

Hours
Daily 5:30pm-3am

Drink Prices
$$$

Food
New American

Nearest Subway
A,C,E,B,D,F,Q to West 4th Street

Credit Cards
All Major

Clementine

1 5TH AVENUE @ 8TH STREET
(212) 253-0003

The revolving door with swimming pool, hotel and gas station icons, spins you into a miraculous potpourri of styles — from oversized, leather-cushioned, 50s-diner sitting arrangements to a 90s wooden bar with cool lines and warm, dim lights. The crowd is just as eclectic, varying from middle-aged diners who follow the chef's renowned cooking, to the downtown business and entertainment set. The later in the evening, the younger and hipper the crowd. The large back room accommodates big parties, and on Easy Mondays, bubbly, hip kids and eternal 20-year-olds pass around lollipops and listen to DJ Shorty's retro music.

Type of Establishment
Comedy Club

Hours
Su-Th 9pm-2am
F-Sa 9pm-4am

Drink Prices
$$$

Food
American

Nearest Subway
1,9 to Christopher Street

Credit Cards
All Major

$5-$12 Cover
+2 Drinks

Comedy Cellar

117 MacDOUGAL STREET
BETWEEN 3RD STREET & BLEECKER
(212) 254-3480

An entertaining downtown comedy showcase without the uptown, flashy commercial texture. You descend the stairs off MacDougal and enter a comfortable club with old-fashioned Greenwich Village dark brick and stained glass decor. Hilarious professional stand-up comedians and the occasional celebrity perform for you on a low stage that is extremely up close and personal. Nosh on some tasty charbroiled burgers, nachos or buffalo wings as you enjoy the show. The delicious array of cappuccino and coffee drinks is also highly recommended. Note: Don't be shy, audience participation is often encouraged and always enjoyable.

Type of Establishment
Club/Live Music

Hours
M-Sa 8pm-4am

Drink Prices
$$

Food
N/A

Nearest Subway
1,2,3,9 to 14th Street

Credit Cards
All Major

The Cooler

416 WEST 14TH STREET
BETWEEN 9TH AVENUE & WASHINGTON
(212) 229-0785

It's dark … it's cold … it's industrial gray … it's a cooler. There are many coolers in the Meat Packing District (hopefully), but none has DJs spinning hardcore, hip-hop or drum 'n' bass every night. This underground bar lends new credence to, 'You never know what's going on behind closed doors or curtains.' Up-and-coming rap groups perform at the Lyricist Lounge party every Thursday, $10 cover. In keeping with the spirit of its location, The Cooler can be a bit of a meat market.

Duplex Cabaret

61 CHRISTOPHER STREET
@ 7TH AVENUE SOUTH
(212) 255-5438

If you love to sing along to loud Broadway
and rock 'n' roll tunes rendered by talented
unknowns (and the occasional headliner)
or just enjoy a blithe, tank-top-clad, red-
cheeked, gay crowd clapping their hands in
ecstasy, wigglin' their hips and smackin' each
other's behinds — this is your place! This
two-floor pub, laid out like a triangle, features cabaret entertainment downstairs with
a wild piano player who beats Jim Carey in
facial distortions, and a laid-back upstairs
where a mixed local clientele plays pool or
chats at the bar. The street cafe allows you to
watch the 7th Avenue scene.

Type of Establishment
Bar/Cabaret

Hours
Daily 4pm-4am

Drink Prices
$$

Food
Bar Menu

Nearest Subway
1,9 to Christopher Street

Credit Cards
Cash Only

The Elbow Room

144 BLEECKER STREET
BETWEEN LAGUARDIA & THOMPSON
(212) 786-4055

This groovy, loungy and cheap nightclub in
the middle of bustling Bleecker Street features
live music seven nights a week. Check out the
bands, hang out at the long bar or in the beat-
up velvet couches and watch Brazilian girls in
tight flower dresses go wild with adventurous
Europeans in jeans on the abused wooden
dance floor. On Monday you can dance to
Brazilian music, from Tuesday to Saturday
you'll get rock 'n' roll, and Thursday is Latin
night. A DJ spins before, between and after
the concerts. The unpretentious, ethnic and
alternative crowd here is having a good time.

Type of Establishment
Bar/Live Music

Hours
Daily 6pm-4am

Drink Prices
$$$

Food
N/A

Nearest Subway
A,C,E,B,D,F, to West 4th Street

Credit Cards
AmEx

Florent

69 GANSEVOORT STREET
BETWEEN WASHINGTON & GREENWICH
(212) 989-5779

Squeeze yourself on scene at the dense diner
tables in this fantastically surreal, 24-hour
Fellini set; admire the ballerina in her baby
blue frills at the deep chrome counter; listen
to a tank-top-clad gay guy's tête-à-tête with
his mother and his lover; but stay away from
the ash-colored Frenchman with his enigmati-
cally smiling blonde from Kiev as he downs a
boudin (blood sausage) and offers you dinner. And when the whole
spook is over, back on
the cobblestones, ask
yourself if you really met
these people.

Type of Establishment
Bar/Restaurant

Hours
Daily 24 hrs

Drink Prices
$$

Food
American/ French

Nearest Subway
A,C,E to 14th Street

Credit Cards
Cash Only

Gonzalez y Gonzalez

625 BROADWAY
BETWEEN WEST HOUSTON & BLEECKER
(212) 473-8787

Type of Establishment
Bar/Restaurant

Hours
Su-Th 12pm-1am
F-Sa 12pm-4am

Drink Prices
$$

Food
Mexican

Nearest Subway
B,D,F,Q to Broadway/Lafayette

Credit Cards
All Major

From the genuine artwork that adorns the pale adobe walls, to the colorful and delicious spicy food, this spot offers that elusive Mexican authenticity long corrupted by the likes of Taco Bell and other south-of-the-border wannabes. Touting the longest bar in New York City, which runs from the front dining area to the rear lounge, Gonzalez y Gonzalez picks up the pace after dark featuring live salsa music Wednesday through Saturday. What's a trip to a Mexican bar without sharing a pitcher of margaritas — blended, shaken, stirred or straight-up.

Hell

59 GANSEVOORT STREET
BETWEEN GREENWICH & WASHINGTON
(212) 727-1666

Type of Establishment
Lounge

Hours
M-Th 6pm-4am
F-Su 4pm-4am

Drink Prices
$$

Food
N/A

Nearest Subway
A,C,E to 14th Street

Credit Cards
MC,V,AmEx

In his *Divine Comedy*, Dante failed to mention that the 10th circle of hell was a swanky martini lounge tucked away in the Meat Packing District. A mask of a bug-eyed Lucifer hangs near the bar — that's only a hint of what you'll look like after you've tasted the Devil's Punch, Lucifer Takes Manhattan, or Fallen Angel. With deliciously potent drinks, comical pictures of celebrities with superimposed red horns, and awesome DJs, this gay-friendly bar is the perfect place to spend the rest of eternity … or at least the rest of the night.

Henrietta Hudson

438 HUDSON STREET
BETWEEN MORTON & BARROW
(212) 924-3347

Type of Establishment
Bar

Hours
M-F 4pm-4am
Sa-Su 1pm-4am

Drink Prices
$$

Food
N/A

Nearest Subway
1,9 to Houston Street

Credit Cards
MC,V,AmEx

A smoky pool table, serious faces framed by short-cropped hair, cigarettes dangling from the corner of thin lips, and sharp eyes following the ball as it disappears into the black hole. The scene could be from *The Godfather* but for one detail: the tough guys are all women. Relax, it's not all that rough at this "Bar and Girl"; in fact, the dark, ancient bar in the front spreads a soothing intimacy which invites singles of all ages and gender to relax with a book as much as it entices lesbian couples to make out at the unlit tables.

Hogs and Heifers

859 WASHINGTON STREET
@ 13TH STREET
(212) 929-0655

Though owners claim it's
sheer coincidence, Hogs and
Heifers is located in the heart of
the Meat Packing District. The
honky-tonk bar, complete with a 1936 hog
(motorcycle) hanging from its ceiling, 138
different specimens of taxidermed animals,
and a collection of bras donated by patrons
that would put Vicki's Secret to shame —
2,533 at last count, guarantees a raucous
good time. Bartenders dressed in Daisy Duke
cut-offs, halter tops, and motorcycle boots,
can be found on the bull horn cursing out
boring patrons or on top of the bar clogging
the night away with the livelier bunch.

Type of Establishment
Bar

Hours
M-F 11am-4am
Sa 1pm-4am
Su 2pm-4am

Drink Prices
$

Food
N/A

Nearest Subway
A,C,E to
14th Street

Credit Cards
Cash Only

Hudson Bar & Books

636 HUDSON STREET
BETWEEN JANE & HORATIO
(212) 229-2642

There's a cozy nook in the back of Hudson
Bar & Books that gives you a hint of its
clientele: on the wall right next to one of the
several ceiling-high bookcases, you'll find a
black and white photo from 1934 of five
men whose combined ages total 434 years.
The average age of the patrons here is far less
than 85 — let's just say this English library-
styled bar attracts an older, more refined
crowd. Enjoy spending the night debating
the misogynist overtones of *Paradise Lost*
and thoughtfully savoring a single malt
scotch … some would say it just doesn't get
any better than this.

Type of Establishment
Bar

Hours
Su-Th 4:30pm-
2am
F-Sa 4:30pm-
4am

Drink Prices
$$$

Food
N/A

Nearest Subway
A,C,E to
14th Street

Credit Cards
All Major

Louisiana Community Bar & Grill

622 BROADWAY
BETWEEN WEST HOUSTON & BLEECKER
(212) 460-9633

Walk in the door and you're instantly cata-
pulted from a restaurant in downtown New
York to a shotgun shack on the Louisiana
bayou. Papier-mâché statues, colored beads
from Mardi Gras and giant crawfish light
fixtures give this Cajun restaurant a festive
feel. Everything from the jalapeño rolls to
the blackened tuna ($18.75) is delicious and
the devilish drinks, like the Hurricane,
Lafayette Lightning, and Mardi Gras Mash,
will leave you feeling like someone put a
great hex on you.

Type of Establishment
Bar/Restaurant

Hours
Su-Th 5pm-2am
F-Sa 5pm-4am

Drink Prices
$

Food
Cajun

Nearest Subway
B,D,F,Q to
Broadway/
Lafayette

Credit Cards
All Major

Life

158 BLEECKER STREET @ THOMPSON
(212) 429-1999

Type of Establishment
Club

Hours
T-Su 10pm-5am

Drink Prices
$$$$

Food
N/A

Nearest Subway
A,C,E,B,D,F,Q to West 4th Street

Credit Cards
All Major

Get in on the steamy scene and dance for your Life. This dance emporium in black concrete has kept decoration and lighting to a bare minimum, since all it's about is dance-dance-dance. A diverse crowd moves in unison to hip-hop, Latin, disco and rap rhythms. Several bars and little tables circle the wide-open arena of physical fun. Bikini-clad girls do contortions on elevated podiums, trying to incite the gladiators on the dance floor. If you've got rhythm and don't mind long lines on the weekends — as fitting for any hot spot in the Village — this is your place to let loose.

Madame X

94 WEST HOUSTON STREET
BETWEEN THOMPSON & LAGUARDIA
(212) 539-0808

Type of Establishment
Lounge

Hours
M-Sa 5pm-4am
Su 6pm-4am

Drink Prices
$$$

Food
N/A

Nearest Subway
B,D,F,Q to Broadway/Lafayette

Credit Cards
MC,V,AmEx

Have you ever been to an erotic bar? Step in from busy West Houston Street into an oasis of…a bordello where you see, feel and breathe red. The whole place appears to be a red-light district, without the sleaze. Instead, comfy couches invite you to put your feet up and as Mimi, the owner says, "This is the kind of place a gal can hang out at alone, without feeling like the biggest loser." On weekends, Madame X is crowded by 10 p.m. so come in advance if you want space. Très cool and mellow. Did we mention that we love this place?

The Monster

80 GROVE STREET @ 4TH STREET
(212) 924-3557

Type of Establishment
Bar/Club

Hours
M-F 4pm-4am
Sa-Su 2pm-4am

Drink Prices
$$

Food
N/A

Nearest Subway
1,9 to Christopher Street

Credit Cards
Cash Only

If you can't find your size, color, class and style in this gay emporium in the heart of the West Village, you're helpless. Whether you prefer the bright, plastic bar and salon with the artificial flowers in the revealing windows upstairs, or the pounding, throbbing and sopping disco downstairs, at The Monster there's something for every gay man's desire.

Moomba

133 7TH AVENUE SOUTH
BETWEEN 10TH STREET & CHARLES
(212) 989-1414

If you're not Madonna, don't even try to get
past the doorman without a dinner reserva-
tion! Once you're in, a deadly cool and stylish
interior, spread over three floors in an intricate layout, awaits. The food looks as attractive as its ultimate decor of exotic plants,
burgundy crêpe drapes and truly beautiful artwork. The hip fashion, entertainment and
nouveau-riche crowd has drinks and appetizers at the seafood bar, dines downstairs or in
the mezzanine, and reposes in the warm,
Asian-inspired lounge upstairs.

Type of Establishment
Restaurant/Lounge

Hours
Daily 7pm-4am

Drink Prices
$$$$

Food
American

Nearest Subway
1,9 to Christopher Street

Credit Cards
All Major

Nells

246 WEST 14TH STREET
BETWEEN 7TH & 8TH AVENUE
(212) 675-1567

It looks a bit stuffy when you first enter, but
Nells — a split-level bar/lounge styled after
an early 20th century English mansion — is
far from boring. The lounge attracts a young,
industry-type crowd that loves great music
and even better, live performances. Teddy B.
(he's the diva with the cowboy hat and long
black ponytail) hosts the amateur talent
showcase on Tuesday nights. "If you come
on my stage you have to be superb," warned
B. "You never know who's watching in the
audience." Prince, Stevie Wonder, Chaka
Khan — the list goes on and on …

Type of Establishment
Bar/Lounge

Hours
Daily 10pm-4am

Drink Prices
$$$

Food
N/A

Nearest Subway
A,C,E to 14th Street

Credit Cards
All Major

Nowbar

22 7TH AVENUE SOUTH @ LEROY STREET
(212) 293-0323

Perfect make-up, hairdos and designer dresses
light up the cave-like walls and mini-water-
falls of this dark grotto. From the black
beauty in sequins with flowers in her hair, to
the leather vamp with silver boobs and the
three Asian girls stroking each other's mane,
they all convince their admirers. Drags and
trendy downtowners come here to adore
each other at theme parties, to enjoy Glorya
Wholesome's drag show on Thursday and
Saturday, or to listen to New York's most
famous DJs such as Sherry Vine, Lily of the
Valley and many more.

Type of Establishment
Bar

Hours
Daily 10pm-4am

Drink Prices
$$$

Food
N/A

Nearest Subway
1,9 to Houston Street

Credit Cards
MC,V

Riviera Cafe & Sports Bar
225 WEST 4TH STREET
@ 7TH AVENUE SOUTH
(212) 929-3250

Type of Establishment
Bar/Restaurant

Hours
Su-Th 11am-2am
F-Sa 12pm-4am

Drink Prices
$$

Food
American

Nearest Subway
A,C,E,B,D,F,Q to West 4th Street

Credit Cards
MC,V,AmEx

This 70-year-old, unhip yet congenial, West Village venue has hidden charm and a refined sense of humor. Squeezed between 7th Avenue and West 4th Street like a ship's bow, a symbiotic downtown crowd hangs at the casual bar with a long front window or at the outdoor cafe (weather permitting). Unusual artwork, such as the *Lady on the Trapeze*, with a head full of coins from all over the world, is perched above the bar. Sports fans venture downstairs to the cozy sports bar hung with 20 TVs, where satellite and cable bring every game of the season.

Ruby Fruit Bar & Grill
531 HUDSON STREET
BETWEEN CHARLES & 10TH STREET
(212) 929-3343

Type of Establishment
Bar/Restaurant

Hours
M-Sa 3pm-4am
Su 11:30am-
    12am

Drink Prices
$$$

Food
Eclectic American

Nearest Subway
1,9 to Houston Street

Credit Cards
All Major

It's one of Melissa Etheridge's favorite spots. Hint #2: Martina Navritolova's picture hangs on the wall. Final Hint: Downstairs in a small glass case are the books *Butch Femme* and *Gay Metropolis*. Still stuck? One more hint: It's always ladies night here. It took you long enough to figure it out Sherlock — Ruby Fruit Bar & Grill is a women's restaurant. The upstairs lounge has a simmering red glow and a 'medieval meets Lilith Fair' feel. Downstairs, the Victorian dining room is candle-lit, cozy and romantic. The fare is American with a twist and you mustn't leave without having the cute crabcakes.

Smalls
183 WEST 10TH STREET
@ 7TH AVENUE SOUTH
(212) 929-7565

Type of Establishment
Jazz Club

Hours
Daily 10pm-6am

Drink Prices
$

Food
N/A

Nearest Subway
1,2,3,9 to 14th Street

Credit Cards
Cash Only

Alcohol Free

Its threadbare banquettes are an eyesore and the candle-lit quarters are extremely cramped (the place lives up to its name), but it's clearly not about aesthetics. The beauty of Smalls is found in the music. Jazz musicians and enthusiasts are typically a nocturnal bunch, so when the rest of the partygoers around the city have passed out, Smalls' crowd is just waking up — which explains why it stays open until 6 a.m., seven days a week. Sorry, there's no alcohol here, only bowls of Chex Mix and pitchers of OJ, H_2O, and milk.

Sweet Basil

88 7TH AVENUE SOUTH
BETWEEN BLEECKER & GROVE
(212) 242-1785

Like the nearby Vanguard, this warm and
lively jazz venue is another well-known New
York establishment. From the Chico Freeman
Quintet to the Spirit of Life Ensemble's
Cuban and Brazilian flavors, there is something for every jazz taste. And whether it's
the jazz freak in rapt attention who suddenly
breaks into loud whaling to a wicked solo,
the quiet corporate couple holding hands, the
black lady at the corner table who turns out
to be tonight's singer or the aging musician in
dark glasses and bandanna, jazz brings them
together. It gets packed as the week grows
older, so reservations are a good idea.

Type of Establishment
Jazz Club

Hours
Su-Th 12pm-
12am
F-Sa 12pm-
1:30am

Drink Prices
$$

Food
Continental

Nearest Subway
1,9 to
Houston Street

Credit Cards
MC,V,AmEx

Terra Blues

149 BLEECKER STREET
BETWEEN LAGUARDIA & THOMPSON
(212) 777-7776

Deep soulful sounds wash over
you as you enter this dark cozy
second-story blues club located
in the heart of The Village. Grab
a seat in the front and look out over the col-
orful bustle that is Bleecker Street, or retreat
to one of the many intimate candle-lit tables
and enjoy the show. It's a mixed downtown
crowd with large numbers of tourists and
NYU students. It packs up on the weekends
so if you want a table arrive early. They offer
traditional blues acts all week long, but they
have been known to experiment with the
setlist on Tuesdays.

Type of Establishment
Bar/Live Music

Hours
Daily 7pm-4am

Drink Prices
$$

Food
N/A

Nearest Subway
A,C,E,B,D,F,Q to
West 4th Street

Credit Cards
MC,V,AmEx

Tortilla Flats

767 WASHINGTON STREET
@ 12TH STREET
(212) 243-1053

We're beginning to wonder what exactly they
put in the tortillas. Most nights at this Mexi-
can bar/restaurant, particularly Hoolahoop
Wednesday (hoop for 3 minutes and win a
free pitcher of margaritas), are of Bacchana-
lian proportions. Former frat boys, sorority
girls and the type of crowd that laces their
sentences with "like" and "awesome" fill
the all-too-colorful room. Tinsel hangs from
every inch of the ceiling, Elvis paraphernalia
covers the walls ... it's 'Graceland meets Animal House.' Loud, kitschy and downright
tacky, but it's an awesome time and like, we
know that you'll love it.

Type of Establishment
Bar/Restaurant

Hours
Daily 12pm-
12am

Drink Prices
$$

Food
Tex/Mex

Nearest Subway
A,C,E to
14th Street

Credit Cards
MC,V,AmEx

Village Vanguard
178 7TH AVENUE SOUTH @ 11TH STREET
(212) 255-4037

What is there left to say about a 60-year-old New York jazz establishment that every aficionado and tourist in this city know? Descend the red staircase into the seductive realm of cool jazz, squeeze yourself into one of the many tables cramping the intimate space, and let yourself be surprised by any type of jazz — from the Vanguard's own 16-man Jazz Orchestra to a flamenco meets jazz event. Photographs of renowned jazz musicians, like Thelonius Monk, and colorful paintings lighten up the dark walls. The attentive crowd takes jazz seriously. So quietly nod or tap your fingers, but please, listening only.

Type of Establishment
Jazz Club

Hours
Daily 8:30pm-4am

Drink Prices
$$$

Food
N/A

Nearest Subway
1,2,3,9 to 14th Street

Credit Cards
Cash Only

$15-25 Cover + Drinks

Waterloo
145 CHARLES STREET @ WASHINGTON
(212) 352-1119

Finally a brasserie that reflects contemporary dining and bar life across the Atlantic. The four owners of Le Zoo — all in their 20s — opened this Belgian eatery over a year ago, and a loyal downtown crowd of locals and avant-garde Europeans appreciate their authentic frites, ambient music and bright, Le Corbusier-inspired design. White and yellow brick walls, white table clothes and red chairs set a nice contrast to hip downtown's black dress code. A camouflage patchwork separates the kitchen from the dining area, which is also divided from the packed bar by a white cloth. It opens to the street in the summer.

Type of Establishment
Bar/Restaurant

Hours
Daily 6pm-2am

Drink Prices
$$$

Food
Belgian

Nearest Subway
1,9 to Christopher Street

Credit Cards
MC,V,AmEx

At times, the East Village appears to be an authentic bastion of modern Bohemia — nourished by a sense of historic beatnik tradition and reinvigorated by 90s chic.

Then again, the area can also seem irreverently pretentious, intimidating and exclusive. But always, the East Village is exciting, shocking and alive.

The area first appeared as a distinct neighborhood in the 60s as artists, fleeing skyrocketing West Village rents, invaded and set up camp. Their radical political and artistic views immediately set this loosely knit colony apart, professing an in-your-face attitude that saturates the neighborhood to this day. Most recently, the area has absorbed large numbers of Latinos, Ukrainians, and gays and lesbians.

An afternoon stroll through the East Village is secondhand shopping at its best, with streets lined with cheap outdoor cafes, music shops and vintage clothing boutiques. Music venues like C.B.G.B. and the Mercury Lounge showcase local talent, while political playwrights hold captive audiences at KGB and Nuyorican Poet's Cafe. The heart of this area's scene, though, is Avenue A and its abundance of bars of all shapes, sizes and persuasions. From the drag queen staff at Lucky Cheng's to the pulsating throngs at Webster Hall, there is something for everyone to experience — at least once.

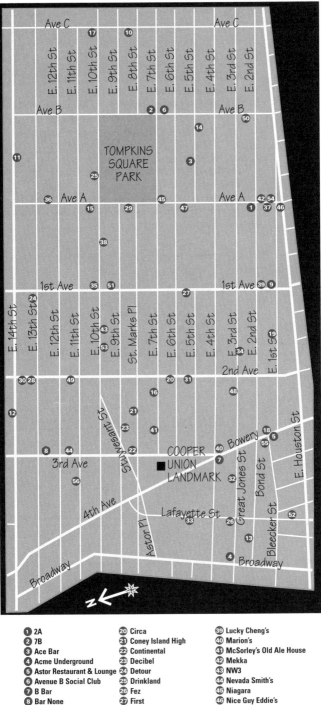

1 2A	**20** Circa	**39** Lucky Cheng's
2 7B	**21** Coney Island High	**40** Marion's
3 Ace Bar	**22** Continental	**41** McSorley's Old Ale House
4 Acme Underground	**23** Decibel	**42** Mekka
5 Astor Restaurant & Lounge	**24** Detour	**43** NW3
6 Avenue B Social Club	**25** Drinkland	**44** Nevada Smith's
7 B Bar	**26** Fez	**45** Niagara
8 Bar None	**27** First	**46** Nice Guy Eddie's
9 Bar XVI	**28** Flamingo East	**47** Opaline
10 Baraza	**29** Flea Market	**48** Opium Den
11 Barmacy	**30** Gemini Lounge	**49** Orson's
12 Beauty Bar	**31** Global 33	**50** Pierrot
13 Bond Street	**32** Great Jones Cafe	**51** Standard
14 Bouche Bar	**33** Indochine	**52** Temple Bar
15 Brownies	**34** Internet Cafe	**53** Tenth Street Lounge
16 Burp Castle	**35** Izzy Bar	**54** Vain
17 C-Note	**36** Korova Milk Bar	**55** Von
18 C.B.G.B.	**37** The Library	**56** Webster Hall
19 Chez es Saada	**38** Liquids	

2A

25 AVENUE A @ 2ND STREET
(212) 505-2466

There's an interesting sibling rivalry going on at 2A. The bar downstairs is like the South, steeped in tradition and leery of outsiders. The lounge upstairs is like the North, welcoming newcomers, trend-setting and modern. Neighborhood veterans, some of whom have been coming to 2A for over a decade, stay downstairs. They set their watches by their favorite bartender's shift, grab a bar stool and order a pint. Upstairs, candles abound and the lights, covered with 30s pinup girls, are dimmed. Patrons laze on leather sofas and order drinks from the service bar.

Type of Establishment
Bar/Lounge

Hours
Daily 4pm-4am

Drink Prices
$

Food
N/A

Nearest Subway
F to 2nd Avenue

Credit Cards
Cash Only

7B

108 AVENUE B @ 7TH STREET
(212) 473-8840

"Remember that scene in *The Godfather II* where the guy gets strangled to death at the bar and dragged into the back? That was filmed here," said Joe who's been coming to 7B for over fifteen years. That scene, *Crocodile Dundee I and II*, and a host of other movies have been filmed at the bar across from Tompkins Square Park. Opened in 1934, the horseshoe bar hails from an era long lost. Joe, affectionately known as the 'Godfather of 7B', hosts Cinema Saturdays — a chance for people to get together, drink Bloody Mary's and watch movies all afternoon.

Type of Establishment
Bar

Hours
Daily 12pm-4am

Drink Prices
$$

Food
N/A

Nearest Subway
L to 1st Avenue

Credit Cards
All Major

Ace Bar

531 EAST 5TH STREET
BETWEEN AVENUE A & AVENUE B
(212) 979-8476

It's across the street from a nursing center, but the Ace Bar is definitely not a haven for the hapless. It's a neighborhood bar with an unwritten rule: tattoos are appreciated. *Rolling Stone* magazine honored the rock bar with best jukebox in New York, with selections from Frank Sinatra to the Beastie Boys. More impressive, however, is the extensive collection of antique lunch boxes worth $50,000 (the Bee Gees box is a must see) that welcomes patrons when they walk in. Sunday brunch features Bloody Mary's and complimentary bagels all day for $2.50.

Type of Establishment
Bar

Hours
Daily 2pm-4am

Drink Prices
$$

Food
N/A

Nearest Subway
F to 2nd Avenue

Credit Cards
All Major

Acme Underground

9 GREAT JONES STREET
BETWEEN BROADWAY & LAFAYETTE
(212) 677-6963

With over 150 different types of hot sauces
on its menu, it's safe to say this Cajun restaurant is one of the hottest places in town.
Taste bud tingling (or torturing, depending
on how tough you are) concoctions like
Heavenly Habañero, Hogs Breath Hot Sauce
and Dat'l Do It Devil Drops line Acme's wall.
Rusted gas station signs make the bar in the
back look like a truck stop only a fat man
named Bubba could love. After a spicy black-
ened dinner, head downstairs for some spicy
alternative rock 'n' roll.

**Type of
Establishment**
Bar/Restaurant

Hours
Su-Th 11:30am-
          11:30pm
F-Sa 11:30am-
          12:30am

Drink Prices
$$

Food
Southern Cajun

**Nearest
Subway**
6 to Bleecker
Street

Credit Cards
MC,V,Disc

Astor Restaurant & Lounge

316 BOWERY @ BLEECKER STREET
(212) 253-8644

Start your evening with a Cosmopolitan at
the marble bar with tin tiles; splurge into
nouveau American/French cuisine surrounded
by a hip and lively up-and-downtown crowd
in the spacious restaurant; then saunter
downstairs to the intricately tiled Turkish
bath-lounge, watch some belly dancing and
clap your hands with hip
Middle Easterners.
Owner Murat Bugdaycay,
has a great sense of
cross-border humor: his
Turkish musicians are
from Greece.

**Type of
Establishment**
Restaurant/
Lounge

Hours
M-Th 6pm-2am
F-Su 6pm-4am

Drink Prices
$$$

Food
American/
French

**Nearest
Subway**
F to 2nd Avenue

Credit Cards
MC,V,AmEx

Avenue B Social Club

99 AVENUE B
BETWEEN 6TH & 7TH STREET
(212) 674-7957

While the flashy decor of many jazz lounges
detracts from the listening experience, the
candle-lit deep burgundy and oak tones at
this East Village hideaway lend themselves to
absorbing the vibes. The club is a comfortable, neighborhood, no-cover jazz lounge
with downtown Avenue B ambiance. Most
nights, live music performed on the centrally
located stage spills over the crowd. The
sounds are usually jazz, but often with a
touch of soul and R&B. There's room to
stretch out downstairs — darker and more
intimate, yet not as polished as the first floor.

**Type of
Establishment**
Lounge/
Live Music

Hours
Daily 4pm-4am

Drink Prices
$$

Food
N/A

**Nearest
Subway**
F to 2nd Avenue

Credit Cards
Cash Only

B Bar

358 BOWERY @ 4TH STREET
(212) 475-2220

It used to be the Bowery Bar and now it's just the B Bar. Though it's lost some its letters, it certainly hasn't lost any of its attitude. The Frankenstein-like guys at the door control the requisite velvet rope and make sure everyone that enters has a 'look.' The voguing can get a little ridiculous and the place can be a bit of a meat market, but once the Boss and Elite model wannabes relax and stop trying to get discovered, a good time is definitely had by all.

Type of Establishment
Bar/Restaurant

Hours
M-F 11:30am-3am
Sa-Su 10:30am-3am

Drink Prices
$$$

Food
American Bistro

Nearest Subway
6 to Astor Place

Credit Cards
All Major

Bar None

98 3RD AVENUE
BETWEEN 12TH & 13TH STREET
(212) 777-NONE

Miss those great college parties? We've found the next best thing. Offering some of the best drink specials in the East Village, Bar None is a high-energy pick-up spot catering to the youngest crowd allowed by law. With just the smallest traces of the East Village, Bar None's up-beat crowd hails primarily from the outer-boroughs and New Jersey, with a sprinkling of the pre-Webster Hall set. Between the well-stocked Top 40 jukebox and the DJ, you'll find something to move to.

Type of Establishment
Bar

Hours
Daily 5pm-4am

Drink Prices
$

Food
Bar Menu

Nearest Subway
L to 3rd Avenue

Credit Cards
Cash Only

Bar XVI

16 1ST AVENUE
BETWEEN 1ST & 2ND STREET
(212) 260-1549

This is not your typical neighborhood bar especially when DJ Franco and his Vampyros Lesbos fly into town. The $7 party gets its name from a Spanish porn flick which helps explain the multi-screen projections of 60s soft-core porn movies that are shown all night. Semi-nude go-go girls take turns tantalizing in a chrome-plated cage. This place drips of sex, but the men aren't sleazy horn dogs — thanks in part to the security guards — and in spite of the gratuitous tits, women do feel comfortable here. If you find upstairs a little too risqué, head downstairs to the mini-bar.

Type of Establishment
Bar

Hours
Daily 8pm-4am

Drink Prices
$$

Food
N/A

Nearest Subway
F to 2nd Avenue

Credit Cards
AmEx

Baraza

133 Avenue C
Between 8th & 9th Street
(212) 539-0811

It used to be a shady bodega that dealt las drogas, but rest assured the only thing this largely huppie and gringo crowd now come to Baraza for is the intoxicating Latin jazz and the great drinks. After having a couple of Caipirinhas, or the equally popular Mojito Cubanos, head to the bathroom and see if you're sober enough to count the number of pennies that cover the wall. Here's a hint: if you can unglue all of them, you'll walk out $375 richer.

Type of Establishment
Bar

Hours
Daily 7:30pm-4am

Drink Prices
$$$

Food
N/A

Nearest Subway
L to 1st Avenue

Credit Cards
Cash Only

Barmacy

536 East 14th Street
Between Avenue A & Avenue B
(212) 228-2240

Don't let the giant jug of bisulfide, pro-phy-lac-tic tooth powder, or distilled witch hazel in the front window stop you from coming in. Barmacy, which was once a pharmacy, definitely has a medicinal charm and the beautiful people love to see and be seen in the bar's banquettes and booths. Ever changing DJs ensure no night at the bar is ever the same. The museum of ancient pills, athlete's foot ointments, and rectal tubes (Lord knows what they were used for) are a little kitschy, but if you're looking for the 'in' crowd, Barmacy is just what the doctor ordered.

Type of Establishment
Bar

Hours
M-F 5:30pm-4am
Sa-Su 7:30pm-4am

Drink Prices
$$

Food
N/A

Nearest Subway
L to 1st Avenue

Credit Cards
MC,V

Beauty Bar

231 East 14th Street
Between 2nd & 3rd Avenue
(212) 539-1389

You can almost smell the hair spray and taste the nail polish upon entering this unique nightspot. Rows of hair dryers and shelves stocked with every feminine hair-care and beauty product imaginable give this spot the look and texture of an authentic salon — not in a trendy commercial pre-fab style, but more akin to that of the local beauty parlor. Unwind with a cocktail Thursday or Friday night while getting your nails done, the only actual service available. It's a comfortably mixed downtown crowd, so here's a chance to find out why women spend so much time getting their hair done.

Type of Establishment
Bar

Hours
M-F 5pm-4am
Sa-Su 7pm-4am

Drink Prices
$$

Food
N/A

Nearest Subway
L to 3rd Avenue

Credit Cards
All Major

Bond Street

6 BOND STREET
BETWEEN BROADWAY & LAFAYETTE
(212) 777-2500

Type of Establishment
Restaurant/ Lounge

Hours
Daily 6pm-2am

Drink Prices
$$$

Food
Japanese

Nearest Subway
6 to Astor Place

Credit Cards
All Major

Downstairs at Bond Street is simply too sexy, whether it's the decor, people or ambiance. Definitely a big winner for the trendy downtown set — it's got all the elements needed for success — celebrity sightings, beautiful women, elegant men and a dark, muted environment. So very New York and so very cool, we're not sure everyone can handle it. But it's not too hard to get a table, which is refreshing, and it's surprising lack of attitude actually makes Bond Street an easy choice any night of the week. Call in advance for weekend nights and dress your best.

Bouche Bar

540 EAST 5TH STREET
BETWEEN AVENUE A & AVENUE B
(212) 475-1673

Type of Establishment
Bar

Hours
Daily 8pm-4am

Drink Prices
$$$

Food
N/A

Nearest Subway
F to 2nd Avenue

Credit Cards
Cash Only

Situated between two dead-end streets, the Bouche Bar proves it's not where you are, but what you are that really matters. For neighborhood people and artists from around the city, the bar is a welcome escape from the tattooed and pierced set that frequents East Village spots. Bouche's loungey, living room decor and amicable bartenders set the relaxed mood of the place. If you don't know everyone in the place when you walk in, you certainly do by the time you leave. "It's the type of place someone can come by themselves and not feel bad," said owner Pamela Caye.

Brownies

169 AVENUE A
BETWEEN 10TH & 11TH STREET
(212) 420-8392

Type of Establishment
Bar/Live Music

Hours
Daily 5pm-4am

Drink Prices
$

Food
N/A

Nearest Subway
L to 1st Avenue

Credit Cards
All Major

The music is loud and the crowds rowdy at this small hard rock dive with a definite downtown feel. Step inside and understand that Brownies is all about the music, and only about the music. Despite the lack of attention paid to the decor the sound system is surprisingly clear — every beat will bounce around inside your head on the way home. Not exactly for the laid back during the week, the crowd's intensity escalates even further on the weekends. While there's no dress code here, it's advisable that you dress down.

Burp Castle

41 EAST 7TH STREET
BETWEEN 2ND & 3RD AVENUE
(212) 982-4576

Gregorian chants and classical
sounds soothe you as you order
a round of ale from an
innkeep clad in the somber
brown robes of a Trappist
monk. Impressive elaborate
medieval murals compli-
ment a decor of immaculate
polished oak. Equally impressive is the selection of beers ranging from the 11oz. bottle of
Arabler at $6.25 to the 3 liter $52.00 bottle
of Corsendonk Brown. Self-proclaimed, "The
Temple of Beer Worship," Burp Castle has
become a favorite watering hole for tourists
and neighborhood regulars alike. Note: The
sign says "No Loud Talking," and the monks
will ask you to leave if you do.

Type of Establishment
Bar

Hours
Su-Th 4pm-4am
F-Sa 4pm-2am

Drink Prices
$$

Food
N/A

Nearest Subway
6 to Astor Place

Credit Cards
All Major

C-Note

157 AVENUE C @ 10TH STREET
(212) 677-8142

"People in the graveyard are feeling you,"
yelled one enthusiastic patron. "My hands are
sore from clapping so hard," cried another.
It's no Blue Note or Village Vanguard, but the
C-Note (and its understated splendor) can
pack them in. Local jazz aficionados love the
place, especially on the weekends. "It takes
me back to the old days when jazz was jump-
ing down here," said a 36-year Lower East
Side veteran. "It's like finding a gold mine on
Avenue C." There's no cover but there is a
one drink minimum.

Type of Establishment
Bar/Live Music

Hours
Daily 7pm-4am

Drink Prices
$$

Food
N/A

Nearest Subway
L to 1st Avenue

Credit Cards
Cash Only

C.B.G.B.

313 BOWERY @ BLEECKER
(212) 254-0983

It's a grungy club held up by old flyers,
posters, and bumper stickers. The wooden
floors are beer soaked and the bar top thor-
oughly battered. It's an eyesore, but it's also
one of the best places to hear rock 'n' roll in
the city. C.B.G.B. has been around for 25
years and everyone from Joan Jett to Sonic
Youth has rocked this stage. Though it's not
nearly as wild as it used to be (those mosh
pit-loving punk rockers are now sitting at
tables and drinking beers), the place still has
an edge and patrons keep coming. Cover
ranges from $3-$9.

Type of Establishment
Bar/Live Music

Hours
Daily 7pm-4am

Drink Prices
$$

Food
N/A

Nearest Subway
6 to Astor Place

Credit Cards
Cash Only

Chez es Saada

42 East 1st Street
Between 1st & 2nd Avenue
(212) 777-5671

Type of Establishment
Bar/Restaurant

Hours
Su-Th 4pm-2am
F-Sa 4pm-4am

Drink Prices
$$$$

Food
French
Moroccan

Nearest Subway
F to 2nd Avenue

Credit Cards
All Major

This soothingly romantic Aladdin's hideout, in an aging East Village brownstone, invites you to dream 1,001 nights away. Have a mint drink at a small bar table, as dim candlelight flickers through Arabian lamps throwing ornate shadows on the white walls and antique photographs. Then follow the rose petals down the stairs, to a mysteriously stylish, colonial catacomb restaurant in Casablanca. Imagine Bogart and Bergman kissing passionately behind the arches as you sink into a comfortable couch and order a delicious Middle Eastern meal. Mingle with an upscale, corporate and hip downtown crowd.

Circa

103 2nd Avenue @ 6th Street
(212) 777-4120

Type of Establishment
Bar/Restaurant

Hours
Daily 11am-4am

Drink Prices
$$

Food
Mediterranean

Nearest Subway
6 to Astor Place

Credit Cards
All Major

'Retro 40s meets the future' in a decidedly hip setting featuring semi-circular booths, a sidewalk cafe, oversized arm chairs by the bar and a DJ spinning five nights a week. The crowd is a glamorous slice of New York's media and fashion elite, the young movers and shakers. But don't be intimidated! There are plenty of 'normal' East Villagers and Upper Eastsiders here too. Circa has an excellent wine list, about 60 well-chosen French, Italian and American reds and whites. Whether you look your best or come in jeans and a t-shirt, Circa is a great place to begin or end an evening.

Coney Island High

15 St. Marks Place
Between 2nd & 3rd Avenue
(212) 674-7959

Type of Establishment
Bar/Live Music

Hours
Daily 5pm-4am

Drink Prices
$$

Food
N/A

Nearest Subway
6 to Astor Place

Credit Cards
AmEx

Clown phobics beware of the menacing joker faces painted on Coney Island High's blood red doors. The rock club, based on the movie *Rock 'n' Roll High School*, has the decadence of Coney Island, but lacks the charm. The carnival theme of this East Village haunt borders on eerie, but it's not quite as scary as some of the rock bands that play here. Covers range from $5-$10 depending on the band. Despite the few punk rock fossils that hover around, it's a fairly young crowd, late teens to mid-twenties.

Continental

25 3RD AVENUE @ ST. MARKS PLACE
(212) 529-6924

Continental is a rock lover's Kmart. Deals, deals, deals. The happy hour from 4-8 p.m. is surprisingly mild, but who cares about a crowd when you've got steals like: five shots of anything for $10, Jagermeister shots three for $5, and frozen Mudslides and strawberry banana daiquiris for only $3. Although management claims that this is a place for new bands to come and test their wings, Iggy Pop, Deborah Harry, Green Day, Guns-n-Roses and a host of other celebs have all performed here. We almost forgot the best deal of all — four to five bands for only $5.

Type of Establishment
Bar/Live Music

Hours
Daily 2pm-4am

Drink Prices
$

Food
N/A

Nearest Subway
6 to Astor Place

Credit Cards
Cash Only

Decibel

240 EAST 9TH STREET
BETWEEN 2ND & 3RD AVENUE
(212) 979-2733

Sink down a few steps off 9th Street and sample the dark forbidding ambiance that surrounds this Japanese sake bar. You enter a small bar area with an ample number of imported sake bottles on tap, before rounding the corner into the main seating area. Its low ceiling and authentic Japanese design work well together to complete the motif. Decibel offers a menu complete with dozens of sake and appetizers (but no sushi) which may intimidate the novice. The amicable staff and friendly atmosphere, however, make this an ideal spot to get your feet wet.

Type of Establishment
Sake Bar

Hours
Su-Th 8pm-2am
F-Sa 8pm-4am

Drink Prices
$$

Food
Japanese

Nearest Subway
6 to Astor Place

Credit Cards
All Major

Detour

349 EAST 13TH STREET
BETWEEN 1ST & 2ND AVENUE
(212) 533-6212

This jazz hideaway sparks memories of grandma's basement — old books here, old records there, old board games like Yahtzee and Christmas lights that have been up way too long. In spite of its dowdy decor, the place is kind of charming. There's no cover charge, instead musicians pass around a tip jar, and the informal environs allow performers to be refreshingly experimental and daring with their music. And there are no black beret-wearing, finger-snapping Bohemians in here. Come in your favorite jeans and sweater and feel right at home.

Type of Establishment
Jazz Club

Hours
Su-Th 4pm-2am
F-Sa 4pm-4am

Drink Prices
$$

Food
N/A

Nearest Subway
L to 1st Avenue

Credit Cards
MC,V,AmEx

Type of Establishment
Bar

Hours
M-Sa 6pm-4am
Su 8pm-3am

Drink Prices
$$

Food
N/A

Nearest Subway
6 to Astor Place

Credit Cards
Cash Only

Drinkland

339 EAST 10TH STREET
BETWEEN AVENUE A & AVENUE B
(212) 228-2435

Psychedelic sky-blue swirls on the ceiling and tables, black and white polka dots on the wall behind the bar and a DJ perched in the corner spinning some obscure track. Nothing to write home about until you escape into the white room in the corner and realize Drinkland does have something different to offer. White leather benches line the white leather walls, white ottomans double as chairs for white tables. The perfect place to drink a White Russian. If white is too sterile, cross the main room and follow the green glow into the ... you guessed it, the green room ... real trippy.

Type of Establishment
Lounge/
Live Music

Hours
Su-Th 6pm-
2am
F-Sa 6pm-4am

Drink Prices
$$$

Food
American

Nearest Subway
6 to Bleecker Street

Credit Cards
All Major

Fez

380 LAFAYETTE STREET @ GREAT JONES
(212) 533-2680

Some places call themselves lounges just because it's in, but Fez has all the reasons to do so. This candle-lit, carpeted Moroccan salon with low tables and pillows is authentic with its cream-colored walls, cushy sofas, and intimate little tables divided by low arches. Savor all this during the week because the weekends are madly packed with cool downtowners. Escape underneath Time Cafe (Fez's upstairs counterpart) and slide into the intimate groove to catch one of Fez's jazz, blues and rock performances. Lastly, don't miss the Mingus Big Band here every Thursday.

Type of Establishment
Bar/Restaurant

Hours
M-Th 6pm-2am
F-Sa 6pm-3am
Su 11am-1am

Drink Prices
$$$

Food
Seasonal
American

Nearest Subway
F to 2nd Avenue

Credit Cards
MC,V,AmEx

First

87 1ST AVENUE
BETWEEN 5TH & 6TH STREET
(212) 674-3823

Love the East Village but tired of theme clubs? Don't have the energy for Karaoke or Improv? May we suggest an evening of conversation, cigars, martinis and late night dining with a distinct urban flavor. Enjoy a smoke while sipping a Cosmopolitan or cognac before retreating to the dining room for a candle-lit dinner. The post-modern decor of brown leather and brick is evenly contrasted by metallic and mirrored surfaces. Flee the bitter competitive reality that is 9-to-5 NYC and join this oasis of after-work revelers. Champagne Sunday Brunch 11 a.m. to 3 p.m.

Flamingo East

219 2ND AVENUE
BETWEEN 13TH & 14TH STREET
(212) 533-2860

Stop in on a Thursday night and howl to the antics of a blathering drunk in drag singing and tap dancing across a stage in a low cut dress, matted blonde wig, and worn down pumps. Introducing Kiki and Herb, the $10 cabaret act that awaits you at Flamingo East. Before you head upstairs to the lounge for a gut-wrenching good time, dinner downstairs in the spacious dining room should not be missed. Entrees range from $11-$18. The Malay Fried Rice ($12.75) is intimidating, but if you ever reach the bottom of your plate, you'll wish the end hadn't come so soon.

Type of Establishment
Bar/Restaurant/Lounge

Hours
Su-Th 6pm-2am
F-Sa 6pm-4am

Drink Prices
$$

Food
Pan-Asian

Nearest Subway
4,5,6,N,R to Union Sq

Credit Cards
All Major

Flea Market

131 AVENUE A
BETWEEN 8TH & 9TH STREET
(212) 358-9282

This quaint French bistro, opened recently on a revitalized Avenue A, has a small bar area with about seven bar stools. A great neighborhood find, the bar is fully stocked and you can order pâté or cheese or even some bigger menu items if you're hungry. A perfect place for two or three people to end up if you don't want to be out till the wee hours and are looking for a cool atmosphere with good music — minus the attitude. A friendly staff with those oh-so-sexy French accents adds to the charm. Mais oui!

Type of Establishment
Bar/Restaurant

Hours
Daily 10am-12am

Drink Prices
$$$

Food
French Bistro

Nearest Subway
L to 1st Avenue

Credit Cards
AmEx

Gemini Lounge

221 2ND AVENUE
BETWEEN 13TH & 14TH STREET
(212) 254-5260

Long black curtains swallow you up as you enter this comfortable dimly lit lounge. Grab a cigar and a Cosmopolitan from the bartender before settling in. Need a breath of fresh air, yet don't want to check your drink at the door? Try the new beer garden out back. That is if you can pry yourself out of the many cozy low-to-the-ground lounge chairs. Soft tones and deep beats mingle with the light cigar smoke most nights. Gemini picks up the pace Tuesdays with its popular Brazilian night and look for the heavy Euro crowd on Techno Thursdays.

Type of Establishment
Lounge

Hours
Daily 5pm-4am

Drink Prices
$$$

Food
N/A

Nearest Subway
F to 2nd Avenue

Credit Cards
MC,V,AmEx

Global 33

93 2ND AVENUE
BETWEEN 5TH & 6TH STREET
(212) 477-8427

Type of Establishment
Bar/Restaurant

Hours
Su-Th 5:30pm-3am
F-Sa 6pm-4am

Drink Prices
$$$

Food
International Tapas

Nearest Subway
6 to Astor Place

Credit Cards
MC,V,AmEx

Crashing, but certainly not burning, into the theme bar explosion downtown is Global 33 — tapping into the pop-culture obsession with anything 60s. Constructed as a 60s-style airport lounge, the decor is a symphony of symmetrical shapes and patterns prevalent in 60s architecture. The DJ directs drum 'n' bass vibes as you enjoy a menu of international tapas and classic cocktails served in shakers. The relatively young mixed crowd probably can't recall being in a 60s-style airport lounge, but all agree it should have looked like this.

Great Jones Cafe

54 GREAT JONES STREET
BETWEEN BOWERY & LAFAYETTE
(212) 674-9304

Type of Establishment
Bar/Restaurant

Hours
Su-Th 5pm-12am
F-Sa 5pm-1am

Drink Prices
$$

Food
Cajun/American

Nearest Subway
6 to Bleecker Street

Credit Cards
Cash Only

Okay, so it's not a big bar and it's mostly a neighborhood joint, but so what? We love the bar at Great Jones Cafe. It's relaxed and mellow; you can actually sit and have a chat with a friend and you don't have to be bothered to look amazing. The bartender actually looks you in the eye, you can order a side of the delicious sweet potato fries and ponder the meaning of life. Perfect for a weeknight venture out with a close friend, if you want one step above a dive. Did we mention cozy and comfortable?

Indochine

430 LAFAYETTE STREET
BETWEEN ASTOR PLACE & 4TH STREET
(212) 505-5111

Type of Establishment
Bar/Restaurant

Hours
Su-Th 5:30pm-12am
F-Sa 5:30pm-12:30am

Drink Prices
$$$$

Food
French Vietnamese

Nearest Subway
6 to Astor Place

Credit Cards
MC,V,AmEx

An established leader among the more upscale eateries on the NoHo scene, this bar/restaurant offers a glimpse into an exotic culture tempered by chic modern influences. Indochine's design is highlighted by giant lush greenery adorning the walls as well as the landscape, strategically and subtly placed so as not to overpower the decor. The fare is French-Vietnamese with a Thai influence, offered up for regular dining as well as an earlier seating for the pre-theater set. There are couples here who have been coming back for years and years, so they must be doing something right.

Internet Cafe

82 EAST 3RD STREET
BETWEEN 1ST & 2ND AVENUE
(212)614-0747

More than just a place to log on, the Internet Cafe is drawing a following for its live music and film screenings. On the surface, it provides a port for techno-nerds to gather; however, like many other non-traditional music venues springing up around the city these days, this spot has developed a reputation for allowing musicians to experiment. The bandstand is located in the middle of this 60-foot-long and 12-foot-wide cafe, forcing the waiter to weave his way between the brass section and the vibraphone while balancing a tray of hot coffee, beer, assorted sandwiches and desserts.

Type of Establishment
Live Music/Cafe

Hours
M-Sa 11am-2am
Su 11am-12am

Drink Prices
$$

Food
Light Menu

Nearest Subway
F to 2nd Avenue

Credit Cards
MC,V,Diners

$10/hr Internet

Izzy Bar

166 1ST AVENUE
BETWEEN 10TH & 11TH STREET
(212) 228-0444

A warm copper glow, not bright but deep and friendly, envelops you as you enter the upstairs lounge. Relax at the bar or slink off into the darker rear lounge to unwind. Then take your time as you make your way downstairs for the live music. The outstanding sound system pumps each chord and rhythm until you not only hear the funk, but you feel the funk. Wednesday night's Deep Trax drum 'n' bass show is the favorite among regulars here. Cover ranges between $5-$10 for live music.

Type of Establishment
Bar/Lounge

Hours
Daily 7pm-4am

Drink Prices
$$$

Food
N/A

Nearest Subway
L to 1st Avenue

Credit Cards
MC,V,AmEx

Korova Milk Bar

200 AVENUE A
BETWEEN 12TH & 13TH STREET
(212) 254-8838

In case its name didn't clue you in, this entire place is dedicated to Stanley Kubrick's 1971 movie, *A Clockwork Orange*. Everywhere you turn there's a naked mannequin … Cultists come in and revel! The Molokos ($7 milk drinks) are heavenly. Moloko Frozen Embryo (coffee-flavored Stoli, Butterscotch Schnapps, Cappuccino Liqueur, ice cream and Snickers bar) and Moloko Karen Carpenter (a banana lover's dream and an anorexic's nightmare) are pure unadulterated pleasure served in a slim glass. You'll have to hit the gym hard after a night of drinking at Korova, but decadence never tasted so good.

Type of Establishment
Bar

Hours
Daily 6pm-4am

Drink Prices
$$

Food
N/A

Nearest Subway
6 to Astor Place

Credit Cards
MC,V,AmEx

	The Library
Type of Establishment Bar	7 AVENUE A BETWEEN EAST HOUSTON & 2ND STREET (212) 375-1352
Hours Daily 12pm-4am	
Drink Prices $$	Booze, books and B-movies best describe this East Village stop. From the classics to pulp fiction, the walls overflow with books to enjoy over a pint. Classic Kung Fu and Monster flicks play on the big screen — the volume off so as not to disturb your read. The classic deep red, green and smooth oak decor provides a literary ambiance, complimented by candlelight. Sorry, the books are only lent out to regulars, but apply for a Library card for reduced drink specials. Note: The librarians at your local branch were never as cute as the ones here.
Food N/A	
Nearest Subway F to 2nd Avenue	
Credit Cards Cash Only	

	Liquids
Type of Establishment Bar/Lounge	266 EAST 10TH STREET BETWEEN 1ST AVENUE & AVENUE A (212) 677-1717
Hours Daily 6pm-4am	
Drink Prices $$$	This cozy and pulsating oversized living room is too good to miss. Best known for their Cosmos, which are truly delectable, Liquids is a great date place. The DJ spins five nights a week, mixing jungle, house or acid jazz depending on the night. Sunday nights are a big couples night. In the winter, there's a fireplace to keep your toes warm. Refreshingly, Liquids is a place that people actually smile at each other. Now when was the last time you heard that about a Manhattan bar?
Food N/A	
Nearest Subway 6 to Astor Place	
Credit Cards AmEx	

	Lucky Cheng's
Type of Establishment Bar/Restaurant	24 1ST AVENUE BETWEEN 1ST & 2ND STREET (212) 473-0516
Hours M-Th 5pm-12am F-Sa 5pm-2am	
Drink Prices $$$	A colorfully loud taste of something alternative doesn't even begin to describe this popular spot with a calling card that reads, "The Original Drag Queen Restaurant." The dirty, drab gray Manhattan streets instantly fade far from view as you step inside and are splashed by the bright kaleidoscope decor. Not only does the dining room feature a full Pan-Asian menu served by a drag waitstaff, but several nightly drag cabaret shows as well. We recommend one of Lucky Cheng's Mini Orgies — the frozen, multi-fruit flavored daiquiris, margaritas or piña coladas.
Food Pan-Asian	
Nearest Subway F to 2nd Avenue	
Credit Cards All Major	

Marion's

354 BOWERY @ 4TH STREET
(212) 475-7621

As kitsch and fabricated as the decor of this 50s wonderland may be, the people running this lovely place are genuine hosts, and the clientele is truly authentic and relaxed. The world of late model and actress Marion is filled with wonderfully tacky mirror drawings, colorful plastic armchairs, flower paintings, JFK and Jackie portraits, even an aquarium with dream castles and blue dogs. Enjoy a martini at the bar or have hearty continental food in the old diner-like restaurant, gently lit by candles and retro lamps. East Village artists, hipsters and trendy downtowners can feel equally at home here.

Type of Establishment
Bar/Restaurant

Hours
Daily 6pm-2am

Drink Prices
$$$

Food
Continental

Nearest Subway
F to 2nd Avenue

Credit Cards
All Major

McSorley's Old Ale House

15 EAST 7TH STREET
BETWEEN 2ND & 3RD AVENUE
(212) 254-2570

Stepping into McSorley's — said to be the oldest ale house in New York — is like going back in time. Sawdust litters the floor, chock-a-block memorabilia and the original 1854 structure invoke the Old Irish in New York. At 2 for $3, even the prices appear to need an update (not that anyone's complaining). McSorley's Special Ale, 2 for $3 and the only alcohol served here, is brewed exclusively for the pub by the old Stroh breweries. Old-World charm, great prices and die-hard regulars make McSorley's a local pub par excellence. Cash only.

Type of Establishment
Bar/Restaurant

Hours
Daily 11am-1am

Drink Prices
$

Food
American

Nearest Subway
6 to Astor Place

Credit Cards
Cash Only

Mekka

14 AVENUE A
BETWEEN EAST HOUSTON & 2ND STREET
(212) 475-8500

When you're in the mood for some great Caribbean or soul food, you've got to make a pilgrimage to Mekka. The bar/restaurant's plantains and honey-dipped fried chicken ($12.95) are just a few of the items on the menu that keep the mixed crowd coming back for more. Even more delicious, however, are the waiters that look like they were beaten with the same gorgeous stick. Customers will definitely want to take them home in a doggie bag. From old funk and soul classics to R&B and hip-hop, the in-house DJ makes sure the music is always moving the crowd.

Type of Establishment
Bar/Restaurant

Hours
Su-Th 5:30pm-
       11pm
F-Sa 5:30pm-
       1am

Drink Prices
$$

Food
Soul/Caribbean

Nearest Subway
F to 2nd Avenue

Credit Cards
MC,V,AmEx

Type of Establishment
Lounge

Hours
Daily 5pm-4am

Drink Prices
$$

Food
N/A

Nearest Subway
6 to Astor Place

Credit Cards
MC,V

NW3

242 East 10th Street
Between 1st & 2nd Avenue
(212) 260-0891

While it may be named for a postal code in London, this is definitely not an English pub. Gauged towards the younger, techno-centric club-hopping set, NW3 is small, dark and engulfed in deep drum 'n' bass vibes. Couches rim the small club surrounding the central candle-lit bar. The checkerboard floor contrasts the black puffy fabric ceiling, but the lights are usually too low to discern any colors anyway. More suited to an intimate get-together than the group thing. Saturdays Deep House DJ selections are a favorite among regulars.

Type of Establishment
Bar

Hours
M-Sa 10am-4am
Su 12pm-4am

Drink Prices
$$

Food
N/A

Nearest Subway
L to 3rd Avenue

Credit Cards
All Major

Nevada Smith's

74 3rd Avenue
Between 11th & 12th Street
(212) 982-2591

Looking for that East Village flavor, but not the annoying East Village pretentiousness? Nevada Smith's is a pleasant collage of the area's charms. The vibe here is high-energy, but in an all-inclusive way. Rather than drawing on just one segment of the nightlife scene, the crowd is a well-blended mix of neighborhood regulars, NYU students, pre-Webster Hall partygoers, and a heavy Euro contingent. Tuesday's Karaoke night crowd is pure energy. Note: Those seeking that ever-elusive perfect pint of Guinness, put this place on your list.

Type of Establishment
Bar/Lounge

Hours
Daily 4pm-4am

Drink Prices
$$

Food
N/A

Nearest Subway
F to 2nd Avenue

Credit Cards
All Major

Niagara

112 Avenue A @ 7th Street
(212) 420-9517

This trendy East Village neighborhood spot has a casually romantic flavor. The corner bar with large windows looking out onto Tompkins Square Park is a comfortable mosaic of deep browns and off-whites, expanded by mirrored reflection and toned by the flicker of aqua-blue lighting. A popular singles' spot, the crowd here is energetic both at the bar area and in the rear lounge. DJs, every night except Sunday, spin a broad selection of pop music. There's room at the bar most weeknights, but it packs up on the weekends.

Nice Guy Eddie's
5 AVENUE A @ EAST HOUSTON
(212) 253-1666

A product of the pop culture reemergence of
everything 70s, this spot is split between
theme bar and Cajun restaurant. Nice Guy
Eddie's caters a full menu of New Orleans
specialties but is taken over by the bar
crowd as the night goes on. The decor is a
mix of black, white and brick with several
TVs and vintage 70s movie posters thrown
in for good measure. The crowd is of the
local variety, but the weekend brings in more
of an outer-borough mix. Note: Check out
the life-size Kiss mural located just outside
on Houston.

Type of Establishment
Bar/Restaurant

Hours
M-F 12pm-4am
Sa-Su 11am-
4am

Drink Prices
$

Food
Cajun/
Southwest

Nearest Subway
F to 2nd Avenue

Credit Cards
All Major

Opaline
85 AVENUE A
BETWEEN 5TH & 6TH STREET
(212) 475-5050

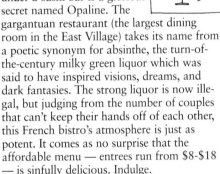

Tucked away from the world
under a sushi bar is a glorious
secret named Opaline. The
gargantuan restaurant (the largest dining
room in the East Village) takes its name from
a poetic synonym for absinthe, the turn-of-
the-century milky green liquor which was
said to have inspired visions, dreams, and
dark fantasies. The strong liquor is now ille-
gal, but judging from the number of couples
that can't keep their hands off of each other,
this French bistro's atmosphere is just as
potent. It comes as no surprise that the
affordable menu — entrees run from $8-$18
— is sinfully delicious. Indulge.

Type of Establishment
Restaurant/
Lounge

Hours
Daily 6pm-4am

Drink Prices
$$

Food
French Bistro

Nearest Subway
F to 2nd Avenue

Credit Cards
All Major

Opium Den
29 EAST 3RD STREET
BETWEEN 2ND AVENUE & BOWERY
(212) 505-7344

Opium Den looks like it could be in SoHo,
judging by the decor — velvet drapes and
candles — and the crowd, in head-to-toe
black. A DJ spins every night of the week,
the bartender is friendly, the crowds relaxed,
and the couches comfy. Try the Cosmopoli-
tans, they're well worth the money. If you
want a seat, come slightly before midnight —
it gets packed between 12:30 a.m. and 1 a.m.
Just get past those velvet ropes on the outside
and you're all set for the night. Leave your
credit cards at home, this is strictly a cash
joint. No baseball caps.

Type of Establishment
Lounge

Hours
M-Sa 8pm-4am
Su 8pm-2am

Drink Prices
$$$

Food
N/A

Nearest Subway
F to 2nd Avenue

Credit Cards
Cash Only

Orson's

175 2ND AVENUE
BETWEEN 11TH & 12TH STREET
(212) 475-1530

Here is a small, intimate yet stylish eatery and bar with a strong East Village accent. Featuring live drag performances Monday and Thursday, Orson's is a popular spot among neighborhood regulars and the occasional tourist. Large globe lights suspended from the illuminated ceiling reflect off the glass-mounted back bar and add just the right touch. Enjoy a taste from the regional menu inside or grab a seat outside in the small front dining area right on 2nd Avenue. Try the variations on the classics like Orson's Cocktail or Orson's Grand Manhattan. No cover for the live drag shows.

Type of Establishment
Bar

Hours
Daily 6pm-4am

Drink Prices
$$

Food
N/A

Nearest Subway
L to 3rd Avenue

Credit Cards
All Major

Pierrot

28 AVENUE B
BETWEEN 2ND & 3RD STREET
(212) 673-1999

One of the latest arrivals on Avenue B is this polished bistro and bar. The decor is Mediterranean-style art deco accented by artistic renderings of Harlequins, not some cheesy animations. Check out the intricate handmade resin bar. The menu is dotted with such delicacies as Prince Edward Island mussels and grilled Bay of Fundy salad. Climb into one of the form-fitting barstools and enjoy a passion fruit Cosmopolitan or fresh strawberry and mango daiquiri. A bright spot on the seedy streets of Avenue B, this place is sure to catch on.

Type of Establishment
Bar/Restaurant

Hours
Daily 6pm-4am

Drink Prices
$$

Food
Mediterranean

Nearest Subway
F to 2nd Avenue

Credit Cards
MC,V,AmEx

Standard

158 1ST AVENUE
BETWEEN 9TH & 10TH STREET
(212) 387-0239

This place definitely has its own set of standards. They don't do much beer, and they don't do blenders. This is not your typical t-shirt and jeans place, it's a self-proclaimed "style lounge" and people usually come dressed. Despite the big attitude from behind the bar, the clientele is not nearly as pretentious. It's fast becoming a favorite among East Villagers weary of the young, tattooed, and pierced set. This hole-in-the-wall is also a lesson in minimalism; no cool art, funky couches, or distractions, just cream felt-covered walls and conversation.

Type of Establishment
Lounge

Hours
Daily 6pm-4am

Drink Prices
$$

Food
N/A

Nearest Subway
6 to Astor Place

Credit Cards
Cash Only

Temple Bar

332 LAFAYETTE STREET
BETWEEN EAST HOUSTON
& BLEECKER
(212) 925-4242

The complex blend of sensual sanctuary and stylish metropolis is so attractive that you want to get sucked deeper into the labyrinthine zig-zag bar. A mural with mystical signs and animals — including the bar's logo, a chameleon — was designed by the late owner Kiki Kogelnic, and separates the brighter and livelier bar from the romantic lounge area. Fine wood, marble and shrill 50s plastic-covered bar stools not only co-exist in this bar, but prove self-assured good taste.

Type of Establishment
Bar/Lounge

Hours
M-Th 5pm-1am
F-Sa 5pm-2am
Su 7pm-1am

Drink Prices
$$$$

Food
Upscale Tapas

Nearest Subway
B,D,F,Q to Broadway/Lafayette

Credit Cards
All Major

Tenth Street Lounge

212 EAST 10TH STREET
BETWEEN 1ST & 2ND AVENUE
(212) 473-5252

Mellow groove tunes wash over the deep oak and polished decor and relax you almost immediately upon entering this trendy lounge. Both the front and rear lounge areas outfitted with stuffed leather couches make this an ideal place for a group gathering or intimate conversation. Its spacious design and ceiling-high plate glass windows overlooking Tenth Street give the appearance of an exclusive uptown club which almost clashes with its East Village crowd. The high black ceiling overshadowing the manila walls, lit by candles and track lights, complete the ambiance encouraging you to forego that beer in favor of something a bit more sophisticated.

Type of Establishment
Lounge

Hours
Su-M 4pm-2am
T-Sa 5pm-3am

Drink Prices
$$$$

Food
N/A

Nearest Subway
6 to Astor Place

Credit Cards
All Major

Vain

9 AVENUE A
BETWEEN 1ST & 2ND STREET
(212) 253-1462

Remember when mother constantly told you to sit up straight because poor posture looked bad and was a sure sign of slovenliness or an impending hunchback? Mother would be happy to know that at Vain the most uncomfortable slabs of wood with leather strips attached to them are passed off as chairs which could cure the most severe case of scoliosis. This place — a chiropractor's dream — proves that beauty is pain and comfort is way overrated. And when you get tired of posing, follow the house and techno beats downstairs; the imported DJs are absolutely amazing.

Type of Establishment
Bar/Lounge

Hours
M-Sa 9pm-4am

Drink Prices
$$$

Food
N/A

Nearest Subway
F to 2nd Avenue

Credit Cards
All Major

Von

3 BLEECKER STREET @ BOWERY
(212) 473-3039

This enigmatic Russian bar seems to be an escaped Czarist refuge. His rescued treasures — an antique bar cabinet with sepia photographs of ancestors behind crystal wine glasses, turn-of-the-century mirrors and heavy picture frames — set the scene for a sophisticated yet mellow lounge. Like in old Russian movies, everything seems premeditated, ambiguous and in slow motion. As an incognito Wall Street suit said, "In New York people want to see and be seen, but I like it here because I can hide and it's mellow."

Type of Establishment
Lounge

Hours
Daily 6pm-2am

Drink Prices
$$$

Food
N/A

Nearest Subway
6 to Bleecker Street

Credit Cards
All Major

Webster Hall

125 EAST 11TH STREET
BETWEEN 3RD & 4TH AVENUE
(212) 353-1600

Enter on the main floor and plunge headlong into a sea of classic disco and pop/rock. Descend to the darker lower-level lounge for a taste of hip-hop and R&B. Catch your breath and climb to the second floor for cutting-edge dance music. Just when you feel that last ounce of energy ebbing away, grab a drink and retreat to the upper balcony to watch the writhing ocean of club kids, tourists and regulars. Psychedelic Thursdays are a little more rock oriented, but dance reigns supreme every Friday and Saturday. Expect to wait on line after midnight and dress to impress.

Type of Establishment
Club

Hours
Th-Sa 10pm-4:30am

Drink Prices
$$$

Food
N/A

Nearest Subway
4,5,6,N,R to Union Sq

Credit Cards
All Major

$20 Cover

SoHo

©ANDRE JUNGEI '98

Originally a commercial district not designated for residential housing, the name SoHo was coined by developers to refer to the neighborhood South of Houston Street.

However, SoHo is not just a geographical location, it is a statement, in which residents and visitors alike proudly stake a claim to being a part of this international hotbed of fashion and art. Known for the small art galleries, sidewalk trendy cafes, and boutiques that line its streets, SoHo is an experience to be slowly sipped, absorbed block by block and savored over an intimate dinner.

Having outgrown its early radical persona, SoHo has carved out a popular niche for itself — culturally and economically. The same lofts once prized for their location, are no longer inexpensive. The escalated cost of living is now forcing up-and-coming artists to flee to Neo-Bohemian enclaves like Williamsburg in Brooklyn, eroding SoHo's cutting-edge reputation. The area's established chic character, however, is firmly embedded.

Bordering SoHo and the Lower East Side, Little Italy remains the heart of New York's Old World Italian culture — a character slowly being whittled away by time. This is where it all started. The turn-of-the-century flood of Italian immigrants into the area's cramped tenements that were the launching pad from which they have achieved great heights. For the most part, though, their aura has moved onward and upward, leaving behind faint wisps of what had been. Still, stroll along the area's storied streets and sample from the specialty shops, restaurants and delightful outdoor cafes carrying on the tradition along Mulberry and Mott Streets.

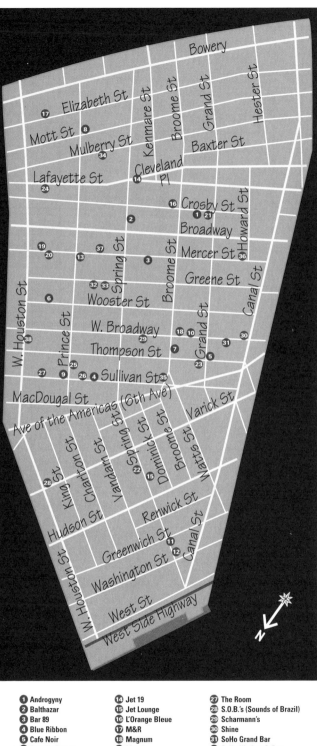

1 Androgyny	**14** Jet 19	**27** The Room
2 Balthazar	**15** Jet Lounge	**28** S.O.B.'s (Sounds of Brazil)
3 Bar 89	**16** L'Orange Bleue	**29** Scharmann's
4 Blue Ribbon	**17** M&R	**30** Shine
5 Cafe Noir	**18** Magnum	**31** SoHo Grand Bar
6 Casa La Femme	**19** Match	**32** SoHo Kitchen & Bar
7 Chaos	**20** Merc Bar	**33** Spy Bar
8 Chibi's Sake Bar	**21** ñ	**34** Velvet Restaurant &
9 Cub Room	**22** NV	Lounge
10 Diva	**23** Naked Lunch	**35** Veruka
11 Don Hill's	**24** Pravda	**36** Void
12 Ear Inn	**25** Raoul's	**37** Wax Bar
13 Fanelli's Cafe	**26** The Red Bench Bar	**38** Zinc Bar

Androgyny

35 CROSBY STREET
BETWEEN GRAND & BROOME
(212) 613-0977

Type of Establishment
Lounge

Hours
T-Th 6pm-2am
F 6pm-4am
Sa 8pm-4am

Drink Prices
$$$

Food
N/A

Nearest Subway
J,M,N,R,6 to
Canal Street

Credit Cards
Cash Only

Dressing Room

Whether you're a professional drag queen, a recreational cross-dresser, a shy New Jersey father of three with secret desires or a boringly straight mortal tired of New York's new impersonal and selective nightspots, this alternative lounge will refresh your senses. Trying to create an all-welcoming community hangout — partners David and Marquesa offer dressing rooms for those not ready to walk around in drag. A pool table helps break the ice between shy patrons, like the stocky guy in a red dress playing against an oversized school girl in a jean skirt, who end up sipping wine together on the couch.

Balthazar

80 SPRING STREET
BETWEEN CROSBY & BROADWAY
(212) 965-1414

Type of Establishment
Bar/Restaurant

Hours
M-Th 12pm-2am
F-Sa 12pm-3am
Su 11:30am-2am

Drink Prices
$$$$

Food
French

Nearest Subway
6 to Spring
Street

Credit Cards
All Major

The hippest, chicest spot in town, you'd have to wait a month for a dinner reservation, unless you're Brad Pitt, or you just walk in with a lot of New York attitude, pretend to have a reservation, flash your card and get really upset if they can't find it — you'll get a table in no time. This warm bistro with meticulously researched French gadgets, such as old mirrors, clocks, and two sirens sensually watching over the bar crowd, offers excellent French food in a fizzing, hip ambiance. The crowd, from fashion to Wall Street, is totally in love with itself and life at Balthazar.

Bar 89

89 MERCER STREET
BETWEEN BROOME & SPRING
(212) 274-0989

Type of Establishment
Bar/Restaurant

Hours
Daily 12pm-2am

Drink Prices
$$$

Food
Eclectic
American

Nearest Subway
N,R to Prince
Street

Credit Cards
MC,V,AmEx

Simple and clean like an Ikea catalogue, Bar 89 is proof that minimalism works. Located in the heart of SoHo, this sleek bar/restaurant is the neo-neighborhood diner. The portions are huge and beautifully presented. Bar goodies like burgers, buffalo wings and nachos look like exotic cuisine. Ever-changing art installations ensure that the space never looks the same. But believe it or not, a trip to the bathroom might be the best part of the evening. So drink up.

Blue Ribbon

97 SULLIVAN STREET
BETWEEN SPRING & PRINCE
(212) 274-0404

Blue Ribbon doesn't win the grand prize for congeniality at our fair, but the neighborhood regulars who frequent the place seem to like it. This compact SoHo restaurant features seafood, but you will also find items like pigeon, fried chicken (and their specialty, attitude du jour) on the menu. In his signature Fila headband, Alonso, the raw oyster bar chef, brings some very needed warmth and personality to this place. Management claims Blue Ribbon has a familial atmosphere, unfortunately we were treated like Stepford children.

Type of Establishment
Bar/Restaurant

Hours
Daily 4pm-4am

Drink Prices
$$$$

Food
Eclectic

Nearest Subway
C,E to Spring

Credit Cards
All Major

Cafe Noir

32 GRAND STREET @ THOMPSON
(212) 431-7910

Some place in Morocco there is a Cafe Noir, but if you don't have the time or resources to go all the way to Africa may we suggest a more suitable option in SoHo. The French Moroccan menu is filled with an array of seafood dishes (entrees $13-$22), colors, and textures. Hand-woven tapestries made of yarn lie on stucco walls. Lanterns covered in faux gems illuminate corners of the room. Gigantic potted palm trees double as incense holders and archway upon archway takes you to an exotic place where knights wrapped in white cloths look stately to the horizon on two-humped camels.

Type of Establishment
Bar/Restaurant

Hours
Daily 11am-4am

Drink Prices
$$$

Food
French Moroccan

Nearest Subway
A,C,E,1,9 to Canal Street

Credit Cards
AmEx

Casa La Femme

150 WOOSTER STREET
BETWEEN PRINCE & WEST HOUSTON
(212) 505-0005

Casa La Femme captures your imagination with its gorgeous Eastern/Maghreb decor. Enter and find your eyes falling to the floor, where people sit on plush cushions around tables and where you can smoke Egyptian tobacco (with apple-cinnamon flavoring) from big hookas. Further inside are tables and chairs, and Bedouin-inspired 'tents,' tables with curtains falling to the ground for privacy. Can you think of a better place for a date? It's low-key and very tasteful. Call in advance for any type of seating. Whether you start or end the evening here, this is a must see for the decor alone.

Type of Establishment
Bar/Restaurant

Hours
Su-T 5pm-12am
W-Sa 5pm-3am

Drink Prices
$$$$

Food
Egyptian

Nearest Subway
N,R to Prince Street

Credit Cards
MC,V,AmEx

Chaos

23 WATTS STREET
BETWEEN WEST BROADWAY
& THOMPSON
(212) 925-8966

Although its name alludes to a
place where wild nights are the norm,
walk through the 25' tall wrought iron
gates and you'll soon realize that Chaos'
clientele doesn't rage, they play. With more
nooks and crannies than an English muffin,
the swanky, palatial, three-level lounge is
prime for intimate conversation and romantic
interludes. Crystal chandeliers, winding stair-
cases, and ever-flowing bottles of champagne
lend a 20s feel to the place. Picture Hugh
Hefner, in a silk smoking jacket puffing on a
Monica that he purchased from the cigar girl,
looking down on you happily drowning in
the plush red velvet pillows that abound.

Type of Establishment
Lounge

Hours
Daily 10pm-4am

Drink Prices
$$$

Food
N/A

Nearest Subway
C,E to Spring Street

Credit Cards
All Major

Chibi's Sake Bar

238 MOTT STREET @ PRINCE
(212) 274-0025

Chibi, the canine namesake of this charming
sake bar, proudly towers in a gold-framed
photograph above the lovingly arranged glass
shelves holding the trinkets necessary for
authentic sake drinking. Mellow, young and
old, hip downtowners enjoy, among others,
7-year-old Koshiyu-Yoshiorino sake in minus-
cule, hand-painted French glasses, and Japan-
ese appetizers at the curved, marble corner
bar. Romantic couples disappear behind the
blue-velvet curtain to smooch at one of the
little tables in the darker, unadorned but cozy
side of the room.

Type of Establishment
Sake Bar

Hours
T-Th 6pm-1am
F-Sa 6pm-2am
Su 6pm-12am

Drink Prices
$$$$

Food
Appetizers

Nearest Subway
6 to Spring Street

Credit Cards
Cash Only

Cub Room

131 SULLIVAN STREET @ PRINCE
(212) 677-4100

A staple of the SoHo bar and restaurant
scene, the regulars at Cub Room call it a
SoHo icon. A yuppy, somewhat older crowd
tends to dominate the scene. The wine list is
exceptional, and they serve a delicious water-
melon martini. Weekdays, everyone comes
suited and booted, lending the place a definite
after-work vibe. But weekends are more
relaxed, although it does feel like an 'Upper
East Side comes downtown' place. We prefer
the early evening scene, when you can actu-
ally get a place to sit and people watch.

Type of Establishment
Bar/Restaurant

Hours
Su-Th 12pm-1am
F-Sa 12pm-3am

Drink Prices
$$$

Food
New American

Nearest Subway
C,E to Spring Street

Credit Cards
All Major

Diva

341 WEST BROADWAY
BETWEEN GRAND & BROOME
(212) 941-9024

Walk down West Broadway and you can't miss Diva. Its doors, a bright fire-engine red, capture the eye and definitely draw attention away from the other more understated places that surround this Italian restaurant. But come to think of it, isn't a diva always supposed to be the center of attention? Its loud exterior is beguiling; however, the candle-lit room is rather sedate. Patrons are too busy enjoying the Ravioli d'Aragosta and indulging in a taste of La Dolce Vita.

Type of Establishment
Bar/Restaurant

Hours
Daily 11am-3am

Drink Prices
$$$

Food
Italian

Nearest Subway
C,E to Spring Street

Credit Cards
All Major

Don Hill's

511 GREENWICH STREET @ SPRING
(212) 334-1390

This place, particularly on Friday nights, is not for the conventional. The party, called Squeeze Box, features scantily clad go-go dancers, drag queens, trannies, homosexuals, and everything in between, all brought together by their love of hardcore rock 'n' roll. The soft porn slide show and movies played throughout the night help set the pace of the evening. "I want people to know that this is a gay nightclub," said promoter Michael Schmidt, "but we have a great mix of all types here."

Type of Establishment
Club

Hours
Daily 10pm-4am

Drink Prices
$$$

Food
N/A

Nearest Subway
N,R to Prince Street

Credit Cards
Cash Only

Ear Inn

326 SPRING STREET
BETWEEN GREENWICH & WASHINGTON
(212) 266-9060

As you've probably already surmised, this place has ears galore. If painter Vincent Van Gogh (the destitute who cut off his ear and sent it to his girl from around the way) were alive he'd love this bar/restaurant. Opened in 1817, this rickety dive was once home to James Brown a reputed black man — go figure — and aide to George Washington during the Revolution. Over the years, this historical landmark has been a boarding house, smuggler's den and brothel. Today, it's a watering hole that has the charm, bric-a-brac and some say ghosts of a cobweb filled attic.

Type of Establishment
Bar/Restaurant

Hours
Daily 12pm-4am

Drink Prices
$

Food
Bar Menu

Nearest Subway
C,E to Spring Street

Credit Cards
All Major

Fanelli's Cafe

94 PRINCE STREET @ MERCER
(212) 966-3518

Type of Establishment
Bar

Hours
Daily 10pm-2am

Drink Prices
$

Food
Bar Menu

Nearest Subway
N,R to Prince Street

Credit Cards
MC,V,AmEx

Fanelli's is old. Really old. The cafe has been around since 1847 and has earned the distinction of being the second oldest continuous food and drink establishment on the same site in New York City. While the rest of SoHo continues to change the 151-year-old corner joint is like an old faithful dog steadfast, reliable and always there.

Jet 19

19 CLEVELAND PLACE @ SPRING
(212) 675-2277

Type of Establishment
Lounge

Hours
T-Sa 9pm-4am

Drink Prices
$$$$

Food
Japanese

Nearest Subway
6 to Spring Street

Credit Cards
All Major

The Balinese wooden masks and delicately woven tapestries that accent the walls give this two-level lounge a South Asian charm. Jet 19 attracts a trendy downtown crowd that likes to snack on bento boxes and groove to classic funk, R&B, and hip-hop. Who wants to sit upright in a boring banquette when huge Balinese daybeds, covered in sparkling afghans, can comfortably hold up to six people laying down? Get there early because the beds fill up fast.

Jet Lounge

286 SPRING STREET
BETWEEN VARICK & HUDSON
(212) 675-2277

Type of Establishment
Lounge

Hours
T-Sa 10pm-4am

Drink Prices
$$$$

Food
N/A

Nearest Subway
1,9 to Houston Street

Credit Cards
MC,V,AmEx

If the old adage about 7 years of bad luck for breaking a mirror is true, the owners of the Jet Lounge definitely won't be getting any good news for a while. Shards of mirrored glass cover every square inch of this place. The glass, coupled with the silver and white color scheme, give an icy, almost igloo-like look to the lounge. You won't find Santa or his elves in this winter wonderland, only fashionable downtowners looking for a cool place to chill (pardon the pun). Watch out, Leonardo DiCaprio, the banquettes resemble icebergs.

L'Orange Bleue
430 BROOME STREET @ CROSBY
(212) 226-4999

La vie est belle at this Mediterranean night spot where the North African music makes even 75-year-old local artists dance on the bar. "Vat can I say!" exclaims Vincent, one of the French owners, as he unbuttons his purple shirt lower and swirls around with a steaming plate of paella. Everything, from the exuberant staff to the warm orange walls and the delicious food, will serve you justice in this world of blue and orange. Monday features Moroccan night with belly dancing and couscous. An eclectic crowd of understated European chic also enjoys the large outdoor cafe in the summer.

Type of Establishment
Bar/Restaurant

Hours
Daily 12pm-2am

Drink Prices
$$$$

Food
Mediterranean

Nearest Subway
6 to Spring Street

Credit Cards
AmEx

M&R
264 ELIZABETH STREET
BETWEEN PRINCE & WEST HOUSTON
(212) 226-0559

This neighborhood gem, on suddenly sexy Elizabeth Street, is just too cozy. We love the intimate feel, casual atmosphere, great scotch selection and the good music in this bar/restaurant. A DJ spins Thursdays through Saturdays. With about fifty varieties per liquor category, ranging from scotch, rum, whiskey, gin, cordials, wine, champagne and brandy, you can easily lose track. A back garden and a back room that doubles as the restaurant offer some seating, but the best place to sit is in the front, right by the bar. They also make excellent margaritas and Campartinis — a Campari martini.

Type of Establishment
Bar/Restaurant

Hours
M-F 5pm-3am
Sa-Su 11:30am-4am

Drink Prices
$$$

Food
Italian/American

Nearest Subway
6 to Spring Street

Credit Cards
MC,V,AmEx

Magnum
357 WEST BROADWAY
BETWEEN GRAND & BROOME
(212) 965-1491

No crazy art deco, no ornate furniture — just cool and simple sophistication with a funky downtown edge. The booths, soft as a suede glove, create the perfect space for a group of SoHo socialites to congregate. The crowd loves to kick back and drink — what else would you expect from a lounge named Magnum? Champagne and great service are not the only things served here: wine, aperitifs, French and Belgian ales, and different treats flow on and on throughout the night.

Type of Establishment
Lounge

Hours
Daily 9pm-4am

Drink Prices
$$$

Food
N/A

Nearest Subway
C,E to Spring Street

Credit Cards
All Major

Match

160 MERCER STREET
BETWEEN PRINCE & WEST HOUSTON
(212) 343-0020

Downstairs at Match is loud, fun and crowded on any weekend night. A real pick-up scene but also a place for a large group of friends. It's great if you have seating, and the food offering is delectable, making for a fine accompaniment to your drinks. The crowd looks like 'Upper East or West comes downtown,' but we don't mind. It's fun here and while not very exciting or innovative for most jaded New Yorkers, Match makes for a good stop on the SoHo tour. Your out-of-town friends will love it too.

Type of Establishment
Bar/Restaurant

Hours
Su-M 11:30am-2am
T-Sa 11:30am-4am

Drink Prices
$$$$

Food
Eclectic International

Nearest Subway
N,R to Prince Street

Credit Cards
All Major

Merc Bar

151 MERCER STREET
BETWEEN PRINCE & WEST HOUSTON
(212) 966-2727

With its colorful oil paintings of American Indians, a canoe hanging from the ceiling, and gigantic black-and-white photographs of a bubbling waterfall, Merc Bar looks more like an exhibit at the Museum of Natural History than one of the hottest night spots in New York. But judging from the crowd, the log cabin motif is working. This bar is perfect for the urban outdoorsy type and even better for those who love good funk, soul and R&B classics.

Type of Establishment
Bar

Hours
M-W 5pm-2am
Th-Sa 5pm-3:30am

Drink Prices
$$$

Food
N/A

Nearest Subway
N,R to Prince Street

Credit Cards
All Major

ñ

33 CROSBY STREET
BETWEEN GRAND & BROOME
(212) 219-8856

ñ (pronounced enya), a dark and sexy Spanish wine and tapas bar, is only inches wide, but endlessly long and barely lit by candles. Squeeze yourself between the exposed-brick wall and the two slim bars in a row, and try to catch a stool to order a glass of Rioja and some tapas (a smart Spanish form of hors d'oeuvres) to keep your alcohol level under control. It gets packed with a rather homogenous Gap and Banana Republic crowd that engages in animated conversations, stays for hours, and seems to love coming back. Cash only.

Type of Establishment
Bar/Restaurant

Hours
M-Th 5pm-2am
F-Sa 5pm-4am

Drink Prices
$$$

Food
Tapas

Nearest Subway
6 to Spring Street

Credit Cards
Cash Only

NV

289 SPRING STREET
BETWEEN HUDSON & VARICK
(212) 929-NVNV

Walk through the dimly lit
corridors and enter a trendy
downtown lounge with
touches of an old world salon.
The glam gods and goddesses who profile on
the vintage chic couches have their fair share
of attitude, but once the voguing ends, which
is usually around 1 a.m., this crowd heads
upstairs and gets down to business: Dancing.
After a few good hours of dirty dancing,
head back downstairs and get to know your
inevitably attractive partner a little better in
one of the sexy curtain-flanked enclaves.

Type of Establishment
Lounge/Club

Hours
W-Su 10pm-4am

Drink Prices
$$$$

Food
N/A

Nearest Subway
C,E to Spring Street

Credit Cards
All Major

Naked Lunch

17 THOMPSON STREET @ GRAND
(212) 941-0479

The bar gets its name from a novel by beat-
nik-era writer William Burroughs. The story
is about a struggling writer who works as
an exterminator to pay the bills. When times
get too tough for the writer and his wife,
they snort roach powder as their sole means
of sustenance. Read the book to find out the
rest, but now you know why the bar's signature is a masterfully designed cockroach. Bug
haters, relax; this Moroccan-inspired place,
is only infested with great drinks, Wall
Streeters, and SoHo Bohemians.

Type of Establishment
Bar

Hours
Daily 6pm-4am

Drink Prices
$$$

Food
N/A

Nearest Subway
A,C,E to Canal Street

Credit Cards
All Major

Pravda

281 LAFAYETTE STREET
BETWEEN PRINCE & WEST HOUSTON
(212) 226-4944

Step down to Moscow's chic
underground, drink exotic
vodka with the terminally fash-
ionable comrades, and act
suave. Something utterly taboo
not too long ago seems to
attract hip New Yorkers, who relax against a
backdrop of Russian street signs and commu-
nist industrial paintings. They are as unpre-
tentiously sophisticated as the scrambled eggs
with caviar served by emaciated Russian
models in black dresses. A friendly, semicircu-
lar bar opens toward a warm, cellar-like
lounge/bistro with atmosphere — well-lit
with candles, well-ventilated, and featuring
jazz as background music.

Type of Establishment
Restaurant/ Lounge

Hours
M-Th 5pm-3am
F-Sa 5pm-4am
Su 6pm-1:30am

Drink Prices
$$$$

Food
Russian

Nearest Subway
N,R to Prince Street

Credit Cards
All Major

Type of Establishment
Bar/Restaurant

Hours
Daily 5pm-2am

Drink Prices
$$$

Food
French Bistro

Nearest Subway
C,E to Spring Street

Credit Cards
All Major

Raoul's

180 PRINCE STREET
BETWEEN THOMPSON & SULLIVAN
(212) 966-3518

On most nights the line to get into this place spills out onto Prince Street. Though it's been around for 23 years, this French bistro is still as popular as it was when it first opened. The front room's familial aura — walls comfortably cluttered with old oil paintings, Victorian era mirrors, and black and white photos — is warm and welcoming. Gentlemen, the ultra-romantic garden dining room is the perfect place to pop the question.

Type of Establishment
Bar

Hours
Daily 5pm-4am

Drink Prices
$$

Food
N/A

Nearest Subway
C,E to Spring Street

Credit Cards
All Major

Red Bench Bar

107 SULLIVAN STREET
BETWEEN SPRING & PRINCE
(212) 274-9120

The magnetic bundle of energy behind the bar is Algerian owner, Mustafa. Everyone calls him Mus (Moose) and he sets the pace of this gregarious and fun-loving environment. Patrons of this small neighborhood place are all Mus' honorary relatives or spouses and by the time you leave, you too will feel like a family member. "This is a very non-threatening place, especially for women," said Lovey, a Bench Bar regular. "You can come in here alone and not feel uncomfortable and you'll be talking to the entire bar in twenty minutes."

Type of Establishment
Bar/Lounge

Hours
Daily 5pm-4am

Drink Prices
$$$

Food
N/A

Nearest Subway
C,E to Spring Street

Credit Cards
Cash Only

The Room

144 SULLIVAN STREET
BETWEEN PRINCE & WEST HOUSTON
(212) 477-2102

Though the bartender believes this fact is trite, The Room is actually two dark narrow rooms, bar on the right, lounge on the left. The industrial concrete and steel setting is quite austere, but neighbors find the place surprisingly comfortable and love the bar. "We don't even consider ourselves customers," said Jane, a Room regular who lives next door, "we're family." You'll find camaraderie, but no Cosmopolitans. There's no room for liquor, only wine and beer.

S.O.B.'s (Sounds of Brazil)

204 VARICK STREET @ WEST HOUSTON
(212) 243-4940

The intimate and colorful tropical ClubMed setting in cool New York envelops a multi-culti crowd of curious Americans, dressed-up Africans, adventurous Europeans, homesick Caribbeans and Brazilians. Get acquainted over a Caipirinha (trademark Brazilian drink) that inspires vigorous and tight dancing to live Brazilian, Caribbean or African music on the well-observed dance floor. After an exhausting lesson on how to shake bundas (behinds) by a snakeskin-clad Brazilian singer, the exhausted crowd relaxes with tropical food at the tables, or back to where it all started — at the elevated bar with a Caipirinha.

Type of Establishment
Bar/Live Music

Hours
Daily 6:30pm-3:30am

Drink Prices
$$$$

Food
Tropical

Nearest Subway
1,9 to Houston Street

Credit Cards
All Major

Scharmann's

386 WEST BROADWAY
BETWEEN BROOME & SPRING
(212) 219-2561

Tired of all those cramped, hustling and bustling SoHo bars, and want to relax with a cup of coffee and a piece of cake, without renouncing people watching to over-decibeled club music? This beige, ballroom-sized Kaffee-haus with exposed fixtures, SoHo artwork, plants and crystal chandeliers is the right place. The hip, beautiful crowd checks each other out across the antique and pseudo-antique furniture, of which each piece is truly unique, including writing desks, lamps and couches. Or, you can lounge around the terrace and watch West Broadway before jumping back into its stream.

Type of Establishment
Bar/Cafe

Hours
M-Th 9am-12am
F-Su 9am-3am

Drink Prices
$$$

Food
Light American

Nearest Subway
C,E to Spring Street

Credit Cards
MC,V

Shine

285 WEST BROADWAY @ CANAL
(212) 941-0900

Shine is a cross between a SoHo chic lounge and a traveling carnival show. *New York Magazine* voted it Best New Club of 1998, but Best Freak Show would have been a more appropriate title. The live entertainment includes everything from contortionists to fire-swallowers, but nothing on stage rivals the giant 6'6" bunny in combat boots that hops (or gallops) around throughout the night.

Type of Establishment
Bar/Lounge

Hours
M-Sa 9:30pm-4am

Drink Prices
$$$$

Food
N/A

Nearest Subway
A,C,E to Canal Street

Credit Cards
All Major

SoHo Grand Bar

310 WEST BROADWAY
BETWEEN CANAL & BROOME
(212) 965-3000

The SoHo Grand Bar shirks the cast iron and glass that typifies the much-reviewed SoHo Grand lobby, and instead embraces wood, warm earth tones, and neutral colors. With the exception of the tables with beautiful elephant tusk-shaped legs, there's nothing too grand about this place. Nevertheless, it's a popular night spot frequented by the likes of Naomi Campbell and Al Pacino. What the bar's decor lacks in personality, it more than makes up for in drinks like the Grand Margarita ($11) and its signature Tartini (Stoli raspberry, chambord, cranberry juice, and a splash of sour mix, $9).

Type of Establishment
Bar

Hours
Daily 12pm-2am

Drink Prices
$$$$

Food
Appetizers

Nearest Subway
A,C,E,N,R to Canal Street

Credit Cards
All Major

SoHo Kitchen & Bar

103 GREENE STREET
BETWEEN SPRING & PRINCE
(212) 925-1866

With over 100 different wines, three 32-spigot cruvinets, and 24 different 'flights' (1 1/2 oz. samples from a group of different wines) SoHo Kitchen & Bar is much more bar than it is kitchen. One of only a few wine bars left in the city, its owner, real estate developer Tony Goldman, likes to think of his downtown diner as the "public library of wine." Check out Flight #9 — destination Southern Hemisphere ($14.75) and try wines from South Africa, Southern Australia and New Zealand. Flight #17 World Class Reds ($42.50) features wines from France and California.

Type of Establishment
Bar/Restaurant

Hours
M-Th 11:30am-
       11:30pm
F-Sa 11:30am-
       1:30am
Su 12pm-10pm

Drink Prices
$$$

Food
American

Nearest Subway
N,R to Prince Street

Credit Cards
All Major

Spy Bar

101 GREENE STREET
BETWEEN SPRING & PRINCE
(212) 343-9000

Spy Bar is notorious for its unwritten, but strictly enforced door policy: if you don't look good and dress even better, you're not getting in here. The new management insists however, that the glam guards and $20 sandwiches are a thing of the past. The huge bar still has traces of its old cabaret days — even the stage is intact. Despite the changing attitude, the crowd remains extremely attractive, and the binocular-like machines positioned in the balcony still make for great people watching.

Type of Establishment
Bar

Hours
Daily 7pm-4am

Drink Prices
$$$$

Food
Appetizers

Nearest Subway
N,R to Prince Street

Credit Cards
All Major

Velvet Restaurant & Lounge

223 MULBERRY STREET
BETWEEN SPRING & PRINCE
(212) 965-0439

This former garage-turned-groovy bar and restaurant, with high ceilings, dramatic red walls and black velvet curtains attracts a high-energy crowd, young professionals from the neighborhood and older folks who enjoy the good continental food. The sumptuous upstairs lounge accommodates large groups on its reupholstered, nouveau-aristocratic couches, and features live jazz on Wednesdays, French chansons on Thursdays and Latin/Cuban tunes on Fridays. All this for no cover charge — check it out!

Type of Establishment
Restaurant/ Lounge

Hours
T-Su 5:30pm-4am

Drink Prices
$$$

Food
Continental

Nearest Subway
6 to Spring Street

Credit Cards
MC,V,AmEx

Veruka

525 BROOME STREET
BETWEEN THOMPSON & 6TH AVENUE
(212) 625-1717

Veruka is the new kid on the 'place to be seen' block. This cavernous industrial-styled restaurant/lounge has a definite 'don't hate me because I'm beautiful and dress better than thou' vibe. Consider yourself lucky — or gorgeous and female — if you get past the doorman. They call it discretion, we call it plain old snobbery; but you can't be 'the place to be' without having a high set of standards: long legs, chiseled chins, designer clothes ... you know, all the important things that fashion magazines are made of. Okay, so we're being a bit catty, but let's hope this place is still in by uhhh ... next week.

Type of Establishment
Restaurant/ Lounge

Hours
Daily 6pm-4am

Drink Prices
$$$$

Food
Nouveau Elite

Nearest Subway
A,C,E to Canal Street

Credit Cards
All Major

Void

16 MERCER STREET @ HOWARD
(212) 941-6492

Surf the net while sipping on Cosmopolitans and check your e-mail while chugging down beers. Void, a multimedia video lounge, has everything from television screens embedded in the banquettes to a computer that features power pellet-gobbling Pac Man. Independent film and video producers, artists and Web designers are welcome to use the giant movie screen to display their work. Check out 'oldie but goodie' movies from the 60s and 70s shown every Wednesday night. "This is not for the mainstream. This place attracts people really interested in creativity," said Taro, a 30-year-old paralegal. Bill Gates would definitely be proud.

Type of Establishment
Lounge

Hours
T-Th 8pm-2am
F-Sa 8pm-3am

Drink Prices
$$

Food
N/A

Nearest Subway
N,R to Canal Street

Credit Cards
Cash Only

Wax Bar

113 MERCER STREET
BETWEEN SPRING & PRINCE
(212) 226-6082

Type of
Establishment
Bar/Lounge

Hours
Daily 5pm-4am

Drink Prices
$$$$

Food
N/A

Nearest
Subway
N,R to Prince
Street

Credit Cards
All Major

Wax Bar is suffused with a sexy, sinister energy that is absolutely infectious. Could it be the wall-length mural that depicts a virile, dark-haired Fabio-type laying on a king-size bed awaiting the pleasure of one of his many concubines? Or could it be the gargoyles hovering over the bar, candelabras illuminating the back area, and blood-purple drapes that all come together to create an ominous lounge that invites you to do and think bad things? Well, let's not get carried away. Anyway, the plush burgundy banquettes in the back are prime for some private 'conversation'.

Zinc Bar

90 WEST HOUSTON STREET
BETWEEN WEST BROADWAY & THOMPSON
(212) 477-8337

Type of
Establishment
Bar/Live Music

Hours
Daily 6pm-4am

Drink Prices
$$$

Food
N/A

Nearest
Subway
1,9 to Houston
Street

Credit Cards
Cash Only

In this live music venue you have no choice but to be at one with the music; the nook in the corner where the bands perform is within arm's length of the audience, but the tight quarters don't stop the jazz bands from jamming every night. Zinc features American and African bands, but the clear favorite among the Mojito drinking patrons are the Latin nights on Thursday, Saturday, and Sunday — $5 cover and a one drink minimum if you opt for a table. If the music's too in your face, follow frisky felines Ella and Holiday (they're cats) into the back room and stretch out.

Lower East Side

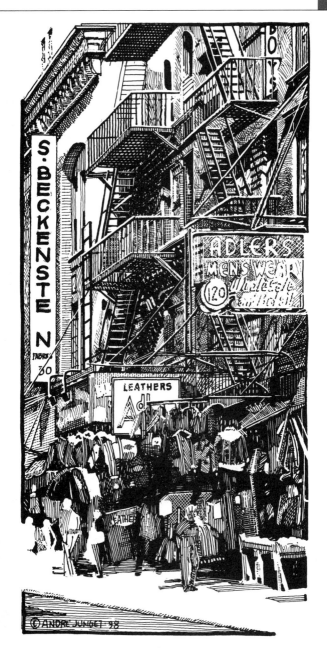

© ANDRE JUNGET '98

Once one of the most overpopulated neighborhoods in the world, the Lower East Side is a swirling reflection of so many influences — past and present.

The Irish, German and Eastern Europeans that once crowded its streets may have moved on, but their presence lingers on in many of the local shops and eateries. Now, primarily Puerto Rican and Dominican immigrants have taken their place in the tenements of Loisaida (the Spanish word for Lower East Side) reinventing the neighborhood as time marches on. The Lower East Side, defined as much by its strong ethnic enclaves as by its large artistic community, is downtown in every sense of the word.

Since the 20s, artists, painters, and writers with politics and prose too radical for even the off-centered West Village spilled over into the Lower East Side. They are drawn not only by the area's aura of urban realism, but its low-income housing and vibrant communal cohesiveness as well. Local area artistry adorning the walls of most night spots attests to this fostering of artistic expression.

The Lower East Side, or LoHo, as some real estate developers are now calling it, is reveling in this resurgence, reflected in the large number of night spots seemingly springing up every month. From the Middle Eastern vibes at Kush to the ultra-swanky Lansky Lounge, there is definitely something going on these days.

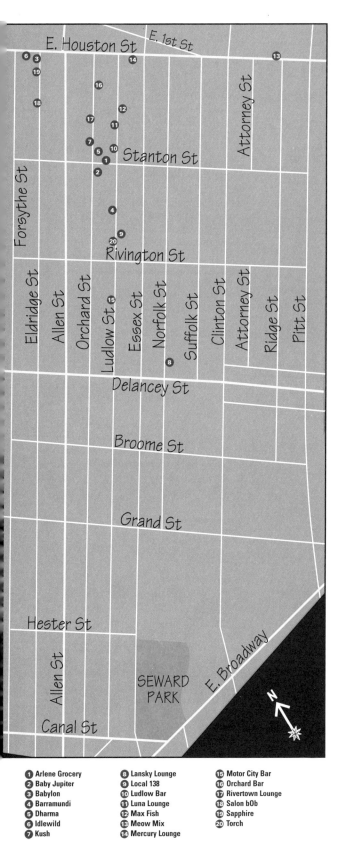

E. Houston St
E. 1st St

Forsythe St
Attorney St
Eldridge St
Allen St
Orchard St
Ludlow St
Essex St
Norfolk St
Suffolk St
Clinton St
Attorney St
Ridge St
Pitt St

Stanton St
Rivington St
Delancey St
Broome St
Grand St
Hester St

Allen St

SEWARD
PARK

E. Broadway

N

Canal St

1. Arlene Grocery
2. Baby Jupiter
3. Babylon
4. Barramundi
5. Dharma
6. Idlewild
7. Kush
8. Lansky Lounge
9. Local 138
10. Ludlow Bar
11. Luna Lounge
12. Max Fish
13. Meow Mix
14. Mercury Lounge
15. Motor City Bar
16. Orchard Bar
17. Rivertown Lounge
18. Salon bOb
19. Sapphire
20. Torch

Arlene Grocery

95 STANTON STREET
BETWEEN ORCHARD & LUDLOW
(212) 358-1633

Type of Establishment	Bar/Live Music
Hours	Daily 7pm-4am
Drink Prices	$
Food	N/A
Nearest Subway	F to 2nd Avenue
Credit Cards	Cash Only

Extremely up close and personal you have the feeling you are in a garage listening to a band perform, minus the mistakes and greasy floor. However, it is its small size that gives Arlene Grocery its charm. The music may be loud, but the quality sound system is such that you are enveloped by the music. The dark atmosphere gives way to a multicolored collage of lights illuminating the band. The crowd is mixed, but as usual there are many Lower East Side local musicians and artists in attendance.

Baby Jupiter

170 ORCHARD STREET @ STANTON
(212) 982-2229

Type of Establishment	Bar/Restaurant
Hours	Su-Th 11am-2am F-Sa 11am-4am
Drink Prices	$$
Food	Southern
Nearest Subway	F to 2nd Avenue
Credit Cards	MC,V

The pale pastel art deco decor is reminiscent of South Beach, Miami-style architecture, but the entertainment is pure downtown eclectic. From comedy to vaudeville and jazz to electronica, Baby Jupiter offers the widest variety of live entertainment downtown and superior acoustic design highlights the effect. The front room is designed diner-style with a lava lamp or two thrown in and features a full menu. Pass through to the main room and enjoy anything from Monday's Improv Comedy to Electro-Fetus party on Wednesday or Mad Groove Saturdays.

Babylon

237 ELDRIDGE STREET @ EAST HOUSTON
(212) 505-7546

Type of Establishment	Cafe
Hours	Daily 9am-12am
Drink Prices	$
Food	Vegetarian
Nearest Subway	F to 2nd Avenue
Credit Cards	Cash Only

Sandwiched between a couple of bars, Babylon is a haven of calm. An eclectic organic veggie cafe offering sandwiches, eggs and soups, Babylon's moderate prices and relaxed atmosphere make it a real gem. Every six weeks Babylon features new artwork on its colorful walls. So if you're looking for a respite from the bustle of the East Village and prefer sipping a cappuccino, beer or wine surrounded by art, Babylon is a must.

Barramundi

147 LUDLOW STREET
BETWEEN RIVINGTON & STANTON
(212) 529-6900

An atmosphere illuminated by candles and deep red lights welcomes you as you enter this trendy downtown bar. Weather permitting, the real party is out back in the spacious garden. A definite downtown atmosphere here is heightened by the conversation of local musicians and artists who mingle amongst the mixed crowd. If the microbrews and cocktails are not racy enough for you, try one of the many house specials including Rough Riders, Two Gals in a Glass, Horn-E-Ania.

Type of Establishment
Bar

Hours
Su-Th 7:30pm-4am
F-Sa 6pm-4am

Drink Prices
$$

Food
N/A

Nearest Subway
F to Delancy Street

Credit Cards
Cash Only

Dharma

174 ORCHARD STREET
BETWEEN STANTON & EAST HOUSTON
(212) 780-0313

Soft sultry percussion slinks out onto Orchard Street and draws you into this comfortable downtown jazz spot. You'll understand jazz is more than music when you see it played in an environment conducive to absorbing every nuance. From the traditional to the experimental, Dharma offers live talent every night except for Sunday. So grab a seat at the bar or fall into one of the comfortable lounge chairs located in the candle-lit lounge areas. And be sure to check out the artwork created by local area artists featured each month.

Type of Establishment
Bar/Live Music

Hours
Daily 6pm-4am

Drink Prices
$$

Food
N/A

Nearest Subway
F to 2nd Avenue

Credit Cards
MC,V

Idlewild

145 EAST HOUSTON STREET
BETWEEN FORSYTH & ELDRIDGE
(212) 477-5005

Your boarding pass here is a 21-year-old face, expensive retro designer clothes, and a determination to look important despite your youthful exuberance. Girly flight attendants serve drinks to kids from good homes who act cool and experienced in this cushioned aircraft imitation. Daughters in pricey designer dresses and sons in 70s shirts flirt to funk spun by a DJ, and chat in airplane seats at the chrome bar, in front of the aircraft's many bathroom doors, or in the tail section, where it gets very smoky. A cylindrical aquarium makes the whole place, kept in icy blue, look even cooler.

Type of Establishment
Bar

Hours
Daily 8pm-3am

Drink Prices
$$$

Food
N/A

Nearest Subway
F to 2nd Avenue

Credit Cards
MC,V,AmEx

Kush

183 ORCHARD STREET
BETWEEN STANTON & EAST HOUSTON
(212) 677-7328

Type of Establishment
Bar/Lounge

Hours
Daily 7pm-4am

Drink Prices
$$$

Food
Middle Eastern

Nearest Subway
F to 2nd Avenue

Credit Cards
MC,V

Step off Orchard Street into the romantic Middle Eastern world that is Kush — where old world music dances with the candlelight. The stucco architecture and ornate artwork and furnishings are complemented by an authentic menu of Middle Eastern delicacies and spirits with a strong Moroccan influence. It's a mixed downtown crowd with a large number of European patrons. Tuesday's Middle Eastern night features a belly dancer, tarot readings, henna painting and a live gypsy band. Tuesday through Saturday Kush offers a DJ including DJ Sasha spinning global fusion on Wednesday.

Lansky Lounge

104 NORFOLK STREET
BETWEEN DELANCY & RIVINGTON
(212) 677-9489

Type of Establishment
Restaurant/Lounge

Hours
Su-M 8pm-2am
T-Th 8pm-4am
Sa 10pm-4am
Closed Friday

Drink Prices
$$$

Food
Eclectic Kosher

Nearest Subway
F to Delancy Street

Credit Cards
All Major

"Down the stairs, through the alley and courtyard, up the staircase, and through the green door. Got it?" said Big John, the imposing dapper don who mans the front door. Open Lansky Lounge's doors and you're instantly transplanted from the late 90s to the late 20s. The old speakeasy takes you back to the days when gangsters like Meyer Lansky were loved and feared, when guys were guys and girls were dolls. Everything on the menu is kosher, so after stuffing yourself with potato latkes, head to the back room and swing the night away.

Local 138

138 LUDLOW STREET
BETWEEN RIVINGTON & STANTON
(212) 477-0280

Type of Establishment
Bar

Hours
Daily 2pm-4am

Drink Prices
$$

Food
Bar Menu

Nearest Subway
F to Delancy Street

Credit Cards
Cash Only

Regulars here in this comfortable Irish/English pub really enjoy drinking with friends in the two traditional snugs (semi-private rooms) located in the front of the bar with windows looking out onto Ludlow Street. The design and soft brown finished wood decor may be that of a traditional pub, but the crowd is certainly a bit trendy. Any respectable pub would not be complete if it didn't offer a superior pint of Guinness, and this spot is no exception — stout drinkers, put this place on your list.

Ludlow Bar

165 LUDLOW STREET
BETWEEN STANTON & EAST HOUSTON
(212) 353-0536

Low ceilings threaten decapitation for anyone 6'2" and over, and with the exception of the gorgeous lamps, the place is not much to look at. The DJs (bless their talented souls) more than make up for Ludlow's decor … or lack there of. Throughout the week DJs spin an assortment of everything from b-side hip-hop to bossanova. The crowd, an eclectic bunch of artists and Lower Eastsiders, relishes this 'come as you are' environment. "This is one of my favorite places to DJ," said Cool Marv. "I can play whatever I want. Ludlow Bar is a DJ's dream."

Type of Establishment
Bar

Hours
Daily 6pm-4am

Drink Prices
$$

Food
N/A

Nearest Subway
F to 2nd Avenue

Credit Cards
All Major

Luna Lounge

171 LUDLOW STREET
BETWEEN STANTON & EAST HOUSTON
(212) 260-2323

Regulars at this spot say it's like seeing a band perform live in your basement, but you've never had a basement like this. Warm reds, glowing oranges and polished brass makes Luna Lounge extremely easy on the eyes. Two or three bands perform a mix of alternative and pop each night except Monday when comedy takes the stage. Local musicians and artists make up only a small part of this mixed crowd and bands end early so that the atmosphere becomes relaxed enough for socializing and drinking with friends — new and old.

Type of Establishment
Bar/Lounge

Hours
Daily 4pm-4am

Drink Prices
$$

Food
N/A

Nearest Subway
F to 2nd Avenue

Credit Cards
MC,V,AmEx

Max Fish

178 LUDLOW STREET
BETWEEN STANTON & EAST HOUSTON
(212) 253-1922

Whereas most downtown night spots display artwork on their walls, Max Fish invites artists to redecorate the entire bar each month. Aside from the pool table, a handful of statues and the curvy snake-shaped bar, little else remains the same from month to month. The artists vary, except for two special shows each year that are neighborhood favorites — a cartoon show and a show displaying the artwork of mental patients. To attempt to describe the ever-changing decor is unfair, except to say the range is somewhere between contemporary realism and psychedelic carnival. Live music offered the first Sunday of every month.

Type of Establishment
Bar

Hours
Daily 5:30pm-4am

Drink Prices
$

Food
N/A

Nearest Subway
F to 2nd Avenue

Credit Cards
Cash Only

Meow Mix

Type of Establishment
Lounge

Hours
Daily 3pm-4am

Drink Prices
$$

Food
N/A

Nearest Subway
F to 2nd Avenue

Credit Cards
Cash Only

269 EAST HOUSTON
BETWEEN AVENUE A & AVENUE B
(212) 254-0688

It's ladies' night every night at this purr-fect alternative downtown local haunt which features live music all week long. The crowd is mostly lesbian, but Meow Mix also taps into the mixed Lower East Side scene on weekends. Pussycat cartoon drawings, leopard skin chairs and numerous other feline features are of interest, but peripheral. The main focus here is on the music and the conversation. Try one of the specials including the Flaming Ho-Moe, Real Love or Troye on the Beach.

Mercury Lounge

Type of Establishment
Bar/Live Music

Hours
Daily 6pm-4am

Drink Prices
$$

Food
N/A

Nearest Subway
F to 2nd Avenue

Credit Cards
MC,V

217 EAST HOUSTON
BETWEEN LUDLOW & ESSEX
(212) 260-4700

The bands go on at 6 p.m. most nights at this East Village nightclub where the emphasis is definitely on the music. From headliners to local talent, this spot features a wide array of artists and musical styles. It's not exactly hard rock, and not exactly easy listening, but there is strong accentuation on local vocals complemented by an exceptional sound system. There's no cover to drink at the front bar, but if you want to pass through the velvet curtains into the heart of the Mercury Lounge where the bands perform there is a $6 charge.

Motor City Bar

Type of Establishment
Bar

Hours
Su-W 7pm-4am
Th-Sa 4pm-4am

Drink Prices
$$

Food
N/A

Nearest Subway
F to 2nd Avenue

Credit Cards
Cash Only

127 LUDLOW STREET
BETWEEN DELANCY & RIVINGTON
(212) 358-1595

The Detroit bar scene has long been a reflection of its neighborly, blue-collar, down-to-earth patrons. Here, in the heart of the Lower East Side, is a slice of that Motor City nightlife. The DJ spins a mix of classic rock tunes, sprinkled here and there with alternative and punk, seven nights a week at this popular haunt for local area musicians. Note: Even though the Detroit Red Wings won the Stanley Cup, Rangers' and Islanders' fans are more than welcome.

Orchard Bar

200 ORCHARD STREET
BETWEEN STANTON & EAST HOUSTON
(212) 673-5350

Wild Kingdom might be a more appropriate name for this bar. With a floor that's reminiscent of rugged terrain, banquettes made of granite, and National Geographic-esque animal flicks playing on a central screen, it's not certain whether one is supposed to grab a drink or pitch a tent. Despite the unnaturally natural look of the place, the staff is congenial and the DJs put on a great show, especially on Mondays. Note: Look for the dripping terrarium in the front window, it's the only way you'll find this place.

Type of Establishment
Bar

Hours
Su-M 6pm-3am
T-Sa 6pm-4am

Drink Prices
$$$

Food
N/A

Nearest Subway
F to 2nd Avenue

Credit Cards
MC,V,AmEx

Rivertown Lounge

187 ORCHARD STREET
BETWEEN STANTON & EAST HOUSTON
(212) 388-1288

Tapping into the revival of Orchard Street is this collaboration of downtown Irish pub atmosphere and uptown chic. The lounge makes the most of the antique turn-of-the-century architecture by combining the texture of an art gallery with the ambiance of your favorite pub. A polished mahogany bar runs the length of the room and faces a lounge area with walls adorned by the artwork of local area artists. A favorite among many Manhattan bartenders, the Rivertown Lounge has DJs most nights, a live blues band on Sunday and never asks for a cover. Note: Busier and much more exciting after 11 p.m.

Type of Establishment
Lounge

Hours
Daily 12pm-4am

Drink Prices
$$

Food
N/A

Nearest Subway
F to 2nd Avenue

Credit Cards
All Major

Salon bOb

235 ELDRIDGE STREET
BETWEEN STANTON & EAST HOUSTON
(212) 777-0588

Regulars at this spot compare it to enjoying conversation and music over drinks in your own living room, only you don't have to cleanup when the party's over. Its comfortable antique decor, bathed in red lamps softened by candlelight, lends itself to meeting friends, both old and new. Sink into one of the cozy leopard skin or blue velvet couches and strike up a conversation with the person next to you who could be anyone from a foreign investment banker to a skateboarder. Various DJs fill out the week — spinning hip-hop, Latin and industrial, with emphasis placed on Sunday's live shows.

Type of Establishment
Lounge

Hours
Daily 7pm-7am

Drink Prices
$$

Food
N/A

Nearest Subway
F to 2nd Avenue

Credit Cards
All Major

Type of Establishment Lounge	# Sapphire
	249 ELDRIDGE STREET
Hours Daily 7pm-4am	BETWEEN STANTON & EAST HOUSTON
	(212) 777-5153

Stepping into this spot you get the feeling of a large nightclub, only on a smaller scale. Flashing strobes and fluorescent bulbs illuminate the crowd dancing to hip-hop, house and R&B. There's a definite downtown Lower East Side vibe here. The crowd is mostly local, but also has a mixed out-of-town flavor. Friday and Saturday features 80s disco and house compilations.

Type of Establishment
Lounge

Hours
Daily 7pm-4am

Drink Prices
$$

Food
N/A

Nearest Subway
F to 2nd Avenue

Credit Cards
Cash Only

Torch

137 LUDLOW STREET
BETWEEN RIVINGTON & STANTON
(212) 228-5151

Torch is a downtown supper club successfully aspiring towards an uptown ambiance. Ornate glowing orange/red wooden fixtures match the larger wall sculpture behind the bar as you walk in. The deep sultry sounds of live musicians are evenly carried throughout the club, providing the perfect appetizer for a menu of French specialties with a South American infusion. Brown suede-textured walls lit by soft golden globes and candlelight make this an ideal place for an intimate dinner.

Type of Establishment
Supper Club

Hours
Su-Th 6pm-2am
F-Sa 6pm-4am

Drink Prices
$$$

Food
French/
South American

Nearest Subway
F to Delancy Street

Credit Cards
All Major

TRIBECA

Like most neighborhoods south of 14th Street, lower Manhattan has changed drastically both geographically and demographically over the past 20 years.

The Financial District, aside from the emergence of the 'city within a city' Battery Park complex, is relatively the same as it was a decade ago. However TriBeCa has experienced significant upheaval, the least of which is gaining identity as a distinct neighborhood. Dubbed by real estate interests to refer to the Triangle Below Canal, the term is actually a misnomer as the area resembles more of a trapezoid. Boundaries began emerging about a decade after SoHo was settled by artists and musicians fleeing the high rents in the Village. Similarly, escalating living costs in SoHo drove the next wave down into TriBeCa. They may have followed the SoHo model in converting the cavernous lofts to housing, but So-SoHo the area is not. The residents are a pleasant mix of young families, ladder-scaling corporates and artists.

Bustling and fast-paced during working hours, the Financial District pretty much sleeps during the night, except for a handful of popular bars and eateries. The majority of the action going on down here at night is in TriBeCa — in its bars, galleries, performance spaces and, of course, the restaurants along Hudson and Franklin Streets — the area's most famous restaurateur Robert DeNiro owns a number including Layla and Tribeca Grill. With the Financial District ever-bulging at the seams, and TriBeCa polishing its nameplate, it's likely the area will grow more cosmopolitan, exciting, and certainly more expensive.

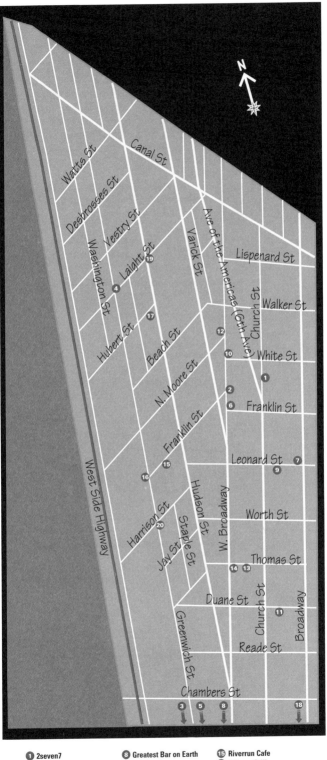

1. 2seven7
2. Bubble Lounge
3. Cafe Remy
4. City Wine & Cigar Co.
5. Edward Moran Bar & Grill
6. El Teddy's
7. Fahrenheit

8. Greatest Bar on Earth
9. Knitting Factory
10. Liquor Store Bar
11. Lush
12. No Moore
13. Obeca Li
14. Odeon

15. Riverrun Cafe
16. Tribeca Grill
17. Vinyl
18. Wall Street Kitchen & Bar
19. Wetlands
20. Yaffa's

2seven7

277 CHURCH STREET
BETWEEN FRANKLIN & WHITE
(212) 625-0505

Once you've found this dreamy TriBeCa hideaway, sink into its cushiony royal-blue couches with padded backs arching to the sky and eat dinner in an open space where walls are playing with warm, flickering candles, hidden flowers and cool, cloudy gray paint. Enjoy the groovy downstairs lounge as you wait for your table, and read the smart, transparent menu against the eye-catching, curved tables which glimmer like fireflies in the dark. The heavenly couches carry you off into the black wall clouds as the DJ spins groove, funk and hip-hop for an upbeat, young and fashionable downtown crowd.

Type of Establishment
Restaurant/
Lounge

Hours
Su-T 6:30pm-
12am
W-Sa 6:30pm-
2am

Drink Prices
$$$

Food
Eclectic

Nearest Subway
A,C,E,N,R to
Canal Street

Credit Cards
MC,V,AmEx

Bubble Lounge

228 WEST BROADWAY
BETWEEN FRANKLIN & WHITE
(212) 431-3433

No doubt, what sparkles here is the champagne. Women in black dresses and guys in Gap shirts with big cigars like to sit in unromantically grouped but aristocratically comfortable couches and chairs and listen to house music while sipping a Le Comte de Monte-Cristo. Brut and Tattinger posters, and high ceilings with lots of fans attract a downtown and after-work crowd, during the week and some 'bridge and tunnel' on weekends. If you want to feel like a VIP, check out the Cru Room downstairs. Live music on Mondays.

Type of Establishment
Lounge

Hours
Su-Th 5pm-2am
F-Sa 5pm-4am

Drink Prices
$$$

Food
Caviar/Sushi

Nearest Subway
1,9 to Franklin
Street

Credit Cards
All Major

Cafe Remy

104 GREENWICH STREET
BETWEEN RECTOR & CARLISLE
(212) 267-4646

Are you one of those suits who, after dark, loves to slink off to the sleazy parts of the Financial District and get down to mambo dancing? A Latino gentleman in a gray zoot and white patent leather shoes will teach you, inexperienced gringa, the essentials of Latin rhythms on the sopping upstairs dance floor. There are some serious dancers at Cafe Remy, and they are a pleasure to watch. Patrick Swayze could've learned some real nasty dancin' here.

Type of Establishment
Bar/Club

Hours
W-Sa 4pm-4am

Drink Prices
$$$

Food
Gourmet Pizza

Nearest Subway
1,9 to Rector
Street

Credit Cards
All Major

City Wine & Cigar Co.

62 LAIGHT STREET @ GREENWICH STREET
(212) 334-2274

Whether you're 20 or 50, come have a
snack at the spacious, cool and functional
bar. Dine on spicy Spanish food in the intimate chef's room or the dining room, or
knowingly dip a cigar in cognac at the
cherry wood cigar bar featuring humidors
and showcases with just about any tool a
cigar aficionado's heart desires. Crowded on
weekdays with business people, and a mixed
crowd on weekends, they all agree on one
thing: cigar smoking is hip. There's a cigar
shop with an international selection, and
wine/cigar lockers for members.

Type of Establishment
Bar/Restaurant

Hours
M-Sa 5:30pm-
2am

Drink Prices
$$$

Food
International

Nearest Subway
1,9 to Franklin
Street

Credit Cards
MC,V,AmEx

Edward Moran Bar & Grill

250 VESEY STREET @ NORTH END
(4 WORLD FINANCIAL CENTER)
(212) 945-2255

It can take you 45 minutes to squeeze by
the animated business suits at Moran. The
corporate world unwinds in this relaxed
pub after another delirious day at the stock
market. The main attraction here, besides its
interminably long indoor space, is the enor-
mous outdoor cafe right on the pier, where
you can watch the Statue of Liberty, big
yachts coming in, a music performance, and
finally the sunset over New Jersey. Four
brunch menus on the weekends and extra
beer stands in the summer keep the crowds
happy.

Type of Establishment
Bar/Restaurant

Hours
Su-W 11am-
10:30pm
Th-Sa 11am-
12am

Drink Prices
$$$

Food
American Bistro

Nearest Subway
1,9,N,R to
Cortlandt Street

Credit Cards
All Major

El Teddy's

219 WEST BROADWAY @ FRANKLIN
(212) 941-7071

You can't miss it: A wickedly colorful airplane (or is it an insect or a big mushroom?)
picks you up outside and lands you in a cool
interior with white Spanish tiles and mosaics,
which, together with Liz Taylor's portrait and
a staff taking itself too seriously, sobers you
up immediately. The fun of Carlos Cas-
taneda's peyote trip is over — but the hip
straight and gay downtown crowd doesn't
seem to notice. They merrily enjoy the psychedelic rock and the 'Naked Lunch monster
insect' tables as much as the exotic margaritas and burritos in the sophisticated bar area,
the diner-like back room, or bustling sidewalk cafe.

Type of Establishment
Bar/Restaurant

Hours
M-F 5pm-12am
Sa-Su 5:30pm-
1am

Drink Prices
$$$

Food
Mexican

Nearest Subway
1,9 to Franklin
Street

Credit Cards
All Major

Fahrenheit (Peppers)

349 LEONARD STREET @ BROADWAY
(212) 343-2824

Type of Establishment
Restaurant/Club

Hours
Th 5:30pm-1am
F 5:30pm-4am
Sa 10pm-4am

Drink Prices
$$$

Food
Cajun/Soul

Nearest Subway
1,9 to Franklin Street

Credit Cards
MC,V,AmEx

Dinner jackets, shiny shoes and long dresses are spiced up with soul, Cajun and Caribbean food, live jazz and blues at Peppers. The long glossy black bar and artworks with an African theme give this spacious locale a Harlem 30s feel, which attracts an upscale New Jersey crowd (free parking lot) and tourists. Fahrenheit, the club downstairs with a strict dress code, offers plenty of dance space and a good sound system. Wednesdays and Sundays are lesbian nights, Thursdays reggae, Fridays comedy or Latin parties, and world music on Saturdays.

Greatest Bar on Earth

WORLD TRADE CENTER 107TH FLOOR
(212) 524-7000

Type of Establishment
Bar/Restaurant

Hours
Daily 4pm-2am

Drink Prices
$$$$

Food
Sushi/Raw Bar

Nearest Subway
1,9,N,R to Cortlandt Street

Credit Cards
All Major

Located on the 107th floor of the World 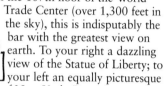 Trade Center (over 1,300 feet in the sky), this is indisputably the bar with the greatest view on earth. To your right a dazzling view of the Statue of Liberty; to your left an equally picturesque panorama of New York. Rest easy, you're not only paying for the view — the live bands, DJs, drinks (sake to Dom Perignon) and food (the sushi is sumptuous) are all worth the trip into World Trade Center Building #1.

Knitting Factory

74 LEONARD STREET
BETWEEN BROADWAY & CHURCH
(212) 219-3006

Type of Establishment
Bar/Lounge/Live Music

Hours
Daily 5pm-4am

Drink Prices
$

Food
N/A

Nearest Subway
1,9 to Franklin Street

Credit Cards
All Major

Do you want to know what's cooking in the avant-garde jazz, indie rock and experimental music scene? Spend a night at this refreshingly unpretentious downtown Mecca of unusual tunes with New York's intelligentsia of all ages. Listen to internationally renowned stars in the main room, free local bands on their assigned weekdays in the Tap Bar, jazz and poetry with film and video at the Alterknit Room, or well-known artists during their 5-night runs in the Old Office, a loungey cigar bar that also features world music on Tuesdays. Or just have a drink at the main bar, rustically decorated with musical instruments made of old farmers tools.

Liquor Store Bar

235 West Broadway @ White
(212) 226-7121

If the group of artist friends at the round table gives you a funny look, it's because you just came from the Bubble Lounge across the street. This friendly and unpretentious neighborhood artist bar, tucked away in an over 200-year-old building, is standing its ground in an exorbitant TriBeCa neighborhood. Get into the groove of warm obscurity, mysterious jazz, and catch a conversation with the bearded writer at the bar, watch the young woman with short-cropped hair and the artwork earrings or the black hipsters in the outdoor cafe. Or just get a beer from the friendly bartender, smoke a cigarette and feel at home.

Type of Establishment
Bar

Hours
Daily 12pm-4am

Drink Prices
$$

Food
N/A

Nearest Subway
1,9 to Franklin Street

Credit Cards
Cash Only

Lush

110 Duane Street
Between Broadway & Church
(212) 766-1295

This resolutely cool and stylish bar with loud house music attracts a decidedly hip, yet relaxed downtown crowd, intent on taking over any promising spot. Once you've found it among the crumbling facades, let yourself be overwhelmed by owner Paul Ujlaky's perfectionist sense for space. He built it all — the impressive cherry wood bar, the upholstered gray walls in the spacious main room with elevated seating areas, a separate lounge for private parties and a small, round, spaceship-like room that serves 25 varieties of bourbon.

Type of Establishment
Bar/Lounge

Hours
W-Sa 5pm-4am

Drink Prices
$$$$

Food
N/A

Nearest Subway
A,C,E to Chambers Street

Credit Cards
MC,V,AmEx

No Moore

234 West Broadway
@ North Moore Street
(212) 925-2595

It may take a while to figure out exactly what's going on in this music lounge, but it's well worth a try. A fun mix of styles in the triangle-shaped top floor with big inviting windows includes a casual arrangement of refreshingly tacky sofas, wooden floors and stained glass at the pub-like bar. In this unhip atmosphere, a relaxed, young, artsy crowd listens to 70s rock and Jimi Hendrix, while concert music is blaring through the French doors. Follow the tunes, and you'll find yourself on a balcony overlooking a live blues band. Venture downstairs and find yourself a table.

Type of Establishment
Lounge/ Live Music

Hours
Daily 5pm-4am

Drink Prices
$$

Food
N/A

Nearest Subway
1,9 to Franklin Street

Credit Cards
All Major

Type of Establishment
Bar/Restaurant

Hours
M-F 11am-3pm
Su-Th 6pm-11pm
F-Sa 6pm-12am

Drink Prices
$$$

Food
Pan-Asian

Nearest Subway
A,C,E to Chambers Street

Credit Cards
MC,V,AmEx

Obeca Li

62 THOMAS STREET
BETWEEN CHURCH & WEST BROADWAY
(212) 393-9887

Cross the wooden bridge into this gigantic Asian temple, and feel important even if you're not Naomi Campbell — who may be dining in the Moongate Room, one of the many chambers and separations generously spread over three floors. Owner Li Ping (Kelly & Ping) knows how to mix ascetic Asian, sleek European and hip New York to give you a feel of sacred privacy in a worldly community. If you like to be part of the fashion and entertainment clan, this is your sanctuary.

Type of Establishment
Bar/Restaurant

Hours
Su-W 11:30am-2am
Th-Sa 11:30am-3am

Drink Prices
$$$

Food
French/American Bistro

Nearest Subway
1,2,3,9 to Chambers Street

Credit Cards
All Major

Odeon

145 WEST BROADWAY
BETWEEN DUANE & THOMAS
(212) 233-0507

This restaurant/bar/street cafe has been around for 20 years and you can tell it's a success — sure of itself and its clientele, it's always crowded. A lively, animated downtown crowd of all ages dines back-to-back in the bistro area, while others chat, smoke and sip a Moscow Mule at the art deco bar. It doesn't take wild decor or loud music to make a place happening — Odeon is proof of that. An understated, sophisticated accent, warm colors and background jazz attract lawyers and judges during the day, suits in the early evening, and the 'fun' downtown crowd later on.

Type of Establishment
Bar/Restaurant

Hours
Daily 11:30am-3am

Drink Prices
$$

Food
Eclectic American

Nearest Subway
1,9 to Franklin Street

Credit Cards
V,AmEx

Riverrun Cafe

176 FRANKLIN STREET
BETWEEN HUDSON & GREENWICH
(212) 966-3894

Be it because "Riverrun" was James Joyce's first word in *Finnigan's Wake*, or that Michael Douglas plotted *A Perfect Murder* here, this rustic English country-style pub, lost on a TriBeCa side street, has a fine poetic air. Hard-boiled eggs and Man Ray photographs consolidate at the cozy bar, while the diner-like area with little separations features paintings by mostly local artists. It gets crowded on Fridays and Saturdays with a loyal, mixed neighborhood clientele. What they appreciate is Riverrun's unpressured atmosphere and its 365 days a year operation.

Tribeca Grill

375 GREENWICH STREET @ FRANKLIN
(212) 941-3900

Only a few doors away from Nobu, this
lively, upscale TriBeCa venue is mostly visited
for its food — the restaurant is always full,
and those at the bar are often waiting for a
dinner table. A big, square space with
exposed brick walls, just the right amount of
artwork and background jazz together with a
friendly, professional staff make for a typical
TriBeCan understated sophistication. A
relaxed, poised crowd of all ages dines to animated conversations around the center bar
(which can feel a little lost with all the action
happening around it).

Type of Establishment
Bar/Restaurant

Hours
M-Sa 5:30pm-11pm
Su 5:30pm-10pm

Drink Prices
$$$

Food
American Grill

Nearest Subway
1,9 to Franklin Street

Credit Cards
All Major

Vinyl

6 HUBERT STREET
BETWEEN HUDSON & GREENWICH
(212) 343-1379

Serious club-goers of all ages and creeds flock
to this alcohol-free party Mecca to get the
ultimate dance experience. The obscure
labyrinth, with acid paintings and strobe
lights, vibrates to the latest groove. Young
hipsters form circles and break it down in the
middle. Stay Fresh with house and jungle
every first Friday of the month, feel Growth
once a month with techno if you belong to
an older generation, float around the Goa
Trance party with hippies in tie-dyes, or get
into a collective sweat to DJ François K's
tunes with a mixed, die-hard dance crowd at
Body and Soul on Sunday afternoons.

Type of Establishment
Club

Hours
T-Th 10pm-4am
F-Sa 11pm-close

Drink Prices
$$$

Food
N/A

Nearest Subway
A,C,E to Canal Street

Credit Cards
Cash Only

Alcohol Free

Wall Street Kitchen & Bar

70 BROAD STREET @ BEAVER
(212) 797-7070

In this temperate two-floor atrium (one block
below the New York Stock Exchange) black
suits relax after closing million-dollar deals.
The clean design, the abstract artwork, the
red walls and orange lamps, and some soft
rock provide the balanced background for a
predominantly male clientele. They even take
off their jackets before ordering a flight of
beer — a sampling of four out of the 100
beers offered. There's also a large selection of
wines, champagne and liquors. Note: It gets
packed on Wednesday and Thursday
evenings, but is closed on weekends.

Type of Establishment
Bar/Restaurant

Hours
M-F 11:30am-12am

Drink Prices
$$$

Food
4,5 to Bowling Green

Nearest Subway
American

Credit Cards
All Major

Type of Establishment
Live Music

Hours
Daily 8pm-4am

Drink Prices
$$

Food
N/A

Nearest Subway
A,C,E,1,9 to Canal Street

Credit Cards
MC,V,AmEx

Wetlands
161 Hudson Street @ Laight
(212) 966-4225

If you're an old or a nouveau hippie with long hair, tattoos and nose ring, or just love to listen and dance to live music in shorts and a t-shirt, this barely lit, two-floor dive-like club offers it seven days a week. Listen to ska or hardcore on Sunday, jungle on Monday, Grateful Dead-type bands on Tuesday, alternative music on Wednesday and Thursday, funk on Friday, and psychedelic rock on Saturday. The management is keen on educating the public about environmental and animal issues by cluttering the walls with political stickers and posters, and a 'VW van turned shop' sells t-shirts, CDs and buttons.

Type of Establishment
Bar/Restaurant

Hours
Su-Th 11am-2am
F-Sa 11am-4am

Drink Prices
$$

Food
Mediterranean

Nearest Subway
1,9 to Franklin Street

Credit Cards
All Major

Yaffa's
353 Greenwich Street @ Harrison
(212) 274-9403

Even if you're not part of Yaffa's eclectic family — white collars, wealthy artists, Europeans and neighborhood kids — Phyllis, the friendly bartender who frequented this 40-year-old bar as a teenager, will treat you as such. Whereas the bar evokes a congenial neighborhood diner, the tearoom overwhelms with its rustic-artsy charm, high ceilings, old window front, and owner Yaffa's self-crafted lamps of fake fruits and crystals that  would have made Carmen Miranda proud. It gets packed with a young crowd on Fridays and Saturdays, and you can tan all day at the popular outdoor cafe.

INDEX

Alphabetical Index

21 Club	Midtown West **28**
2A	East Village **90**
2i's	Greenwich Village **74**
2seven7	TriBeCa **138**
4₂0	Upper West Side **12**
44 (Royalton)	Midtown West **28**
55 Bar	Greenwich Village **74**
5757 (Four Seasons)	Midtown East **42**
7B	East Village **90**
Ace Bar	East Village **90**
Acme Underground	East Village **91**
American Trash	Upper East Side **20**
Androgyny	SoHo **112**
Aquavit	Midtown West **28**
Arlene Grocery	Lower East Side **128**
Art Bar	Greenwich Village **74**
Asia de Cuba	Midtown East **42**
Astor Restaurant & Lounge	East Village **91**
Au Bar	Midtown East **42**
Aubette	Gramercy **64**
Auction House	Upper East Side **20**
Avenue B Social Club	East Village **91**
B Bar	East Village **92**
B. Smith's	Midtown West **29**
Baby Jupiter	Lower East Side **128**
Babylon	Lower East Side **128**
Bahi	Gramercy **64**
Baktun	Chelsea **52**
Balthazar	SoHo **112**
Bar 54	Midtown West **29**
Bar 89	SoHo **112**
Bar D'O	Greenwich Village **75**
Bar Nine	Midtown West **29**
Bar None	East Village **92**
Bar Six	Greenwich Village **75**
Bar XVI	East Village **92**
Baraza	East Village **93**
Barmacy	East Village **page 93**
Barracuda	Chelsea **page 52**
Barramundi	Lower East Side **129**
Beauty Bar	East Village **93**
Beekman Bar & Books	Midtown East **43**
Belmont Lounge	Gramercy **64**
Big Sur	Upper East Side **20**
Bill's Gay Nineties	Midtown East **43**
Birdland	Midtown West **30**
Bistro Latino	Midtown West **30**
Bitter End	Greenwich Village **75**
Blue Note	Greenwich Village **76**
Blue Ribbon	SoHo **113**
Blue Water Grill	Gramercy **65**
Bond Street	East Village **94**
Boston Comedy Club	Greenwich Village **76**
Bottom Line	Greenwich Village **76**
Bouche Bar	East Village **94**

Braque	Greenwich Village **77**
Brother Jimmy's	Upper East Side **21**
Brownies	East Village **94**
Bryant Park Grill	Midtown West **30**
Bubble Lounge	TriBeCa **138**
Bull & Bear (Waldorf-Astoria)	Midtown East **43**
Burp Castle	East Village **95**
C-Note	East Village **95**
C.B.G.B.	East Village **95**
Cafe Carlyle (Carlyle Hotel)	Upper East Side **21**
Cafe Lalo	Upper West Side **12**
Cafe Noir	SoHo **113**
Cafe Pappagallo	Midtown West **31**
Cafe Remy	TriBeCa **138**
Cafe Wha?	Greenwich Village **77**
Cafeteria	Chelsea **52**
Caroline's	Midtown West **31**
Casa La Femme	SoHo **113**
Chaos	SoHo **114**
Cheetah	Chelsea **53**
Chez es Saada	East Village **96**
Chibi's Sake Bar	SoHo **114**
Chicago B.L.U.E.S.	Greenwich Village **77**
China Club	Midtown West **31**
Cibar (Inn at Irving Place)	Gramercy **65**
Ciel Rouge	Chelsea **53**
Circa	East Village **96**
Citrus Bar & Grill	Upper West Side **12**
City Wine & Cigar Co.	TriBeCa **139**
Clementine	Greenwich Village **78**
Cleopatra's Needle	Upper West Side **13**
Club Macanudo	Upper East Side **21**
Coffee Shop	Gramercy **65**
Comedy Cellar	Greenwich Village **78**
Commonwealth Brewery	Midtown West **32**
Coney Island High	East Village **96**
Continental	East Village **97**
The Cooler	Greenwich Village **78**
Copacabana	Midtown West **32**
Cub Room	SoHo **114**
DT-UT	Upper East Side **22**
Decibel	East Village **97**
Denim & Diamonds	Midtown East **44**
Detour	East Village **97**
Dharma	Lower East Side **129**
Diva	SoHo **115**
Divine Bar	Midtown East **44**
Don Hill's	SoHo **115**
Don't Tell Mama	Midtown West **32**
Downtime	Chelsea **53**
Drinkland	East Village **98**
Duplex Cabaret	Greenwich Village **79**
Dusk	Chelsea **54**
Ear Inn	SoHo **115**
East of 8th	Chelsea **54**

Edward Moran Bar & Grill	TriBeCa	**139**
El Flamingo	Chelsea	**54**
El Teddy's	TriBeCa	**139**
Elbow Room	Greenwich Village	**79**
Exile	Upper West Side	**13**
Fahrenheit	TriBeCa	**140**
Fanelli's Cafe	SoHo	**116**
Fez	East Village	**98**
Film Center Cafe	Midtown West	**33**
First	East Village	**98**
Flamingo East	East Village	**99**
Flea Market	East Village	**99**
Florent	Greenwich Village	**79**
Flowers	Chelsea	**55**
Flute	Midtown West	**33**
Fred's Beauty Bar	Chelsea	**55**
G Lounge	Chelsea	**55**
Gemini Lounge	East Village	**99**
Global 33	East Village	**100**
Gonzalez y Gonzalez	Greenwich Village	**80**
Gramercy Park Hotel	Gramercy	**66**
Gramercy Tavern	Gramercy	**66**
Great Jones Cafe	East Village	**100**
Greatest Bar on Earth	TriBeCa	**140**
Hammerstein Ballroom	Chelsea	**56**
Heartland Brewery	Gramercy	**66**
Hell	Greenwich Village	**80**
Henrietta Hudson	Greenwich Village	**80**
Hi-Life Bar & Grill	Upper West Side	**13**
Hi-Life Rest. & Lounge	Upper East Side	**22**
Hogs & Heifers	Greenwich Village	**81**
Hudson Bar & Books	Greenwich Village	**81**
Idlewild	Lower East Side	**129**
Indigo	Upper West Side	**14**
Indochine	East Village	**100**
Internet Cafe	East Village	**101**
Iridium (Empire Hotel)	Upper West Side	**14**
Irving Plaza	Gramercy	**67**
Izzy Bar	East Village	**101**
Jazz Standard	Gramercy	**67**
Jet 19	SoHo	**116**
Jet Lounge	SoHo	**116**
Jezebel	Midtown West	**33**
Joshua Tree	Gramercy	**67**
Journey's Lounge (Essex House)	Midtown West	**34**
Julie's	Midtown East	**44**
Justin's	Chelsea	**56**
Kashmir	Gramercy	**68**
King Cole Bar (St. Regis)	Midtown East	**45**
Kit Kat Klub	Midtown West	**34**
Knitting Factory	TriBeCa	**140**
Korova Milk Bar	East Village	**101**
Kush	Lower East Side	**130**
La Maison de Sade	Chelsea	**56**
La Nueva Escuelita	Midtown West	**34**

Louisiana Community Bar & Grill	Greenwich Village **81**
Lansky Lounge	Lower East Side **130**
Le Bar Bat	Midtown West **35**
Lemon	Gramercy **68**
Lexington Bar & Books	Upper East Side **22**
The Library	East Village **102**
Life	Greenwich Village **82**
Liquids	East Village **102**
Liquor Store Bar	TriBeCa **141**
Local 138	Lower East Side **130**
Lola	Chelsea **57**
L'Orange Bleue	SoHo **117**
Lot 61	Chelsea **57**
Lucky Cheng's	East Village **102**
Ludlow Bar	Lower East Side **131**
Luna Lounge	Lower East Side **131**
Luna Park	Gramercy **68**
Lush	TriBeCa **141**
M & R	SoHo **117**
Madame X	Greenwich Village **82**
Magnum	SoHo **117**
Manny's Car Wash	Upper East Side **23**
Marion's	East Village **103**
Martell's	Upper East Side **23**
Match	SoHo **118**
Match-Uptown	Midtown East **45**
Max Fish	Lower East Side **131**
McSorley's Old Ale House	East Village **103**
Mekka	East Village **103**
Meow Mix	Lower East Side **132**
Merc Bar	SoHo **118**
Merchants NY	Upper West Side **14**
Merchants NY	Upper East Side **23**
Merchants NY	Chelsea **57**
Mercury Lounge	Lower East Side **132**
Metronome	Gramercy **69**
Mimosa	Chelsea **58**
Monkey Bar (Hotel Elysee)	Midtown East **45**
Monster	Greenwich Village **82**
Moomba	Greenwich Village **83**
Moonlightling	Upper West Side **15**
Morgan's (Morgan Hotel)	Midtown East **46**
Moscow	Midtown East **46**
Mother	Chelsea **58**
Motor City Bar	Lower East Side **132**
ñ	SoHo **118**
NV	SoHo **119**
NW3	East Village **104**
Naked Lunch	SoHo **119**
Nells	Greenwich Village **83**
Nevada Smith's	East Village **104**
Niagara	East Village **104**
Nice Guy Eddie's	East Village **105**
No Moore	TriBeCa **141**
Nowbar	Greenwich Village **83**

Alphabetical Index (continued)

Oak Room (Algonquin Hotel)	Midtown West **35**
Oak Room (Plaza Hotel)	Midtown East **46**
Obeca Li	TriBeCa **142**
Odeon	TriBeCa **142**
Ohm	Chelsea **58**
Opaline	East Village **105**
Opera	Chelsea **59**
Opium Den	East Village **105**
Orchard Bar	Lower East Side **133**
Orson's	East Village **106**
Pete's Tavern	Gramercy **69**
Pierrot	East Village **106**
Pravda	SoHo **119**
Prohibition	Upper West Side **15**
Punch	Gramercy **69**
Raoul's	SoHo **120**
Rebar	Chelsea **59**
Red Bench Bar	SoHo **120**
Republic	Gramercy **70**
Revolution	Midtown West **35**
Riverrun Cafe	TriBeCa **142**
Rivertown Lounge	Lower East Side **133**
Riviera Cafe & Sports Bar	Greenwich Village **84**
The Room	SoHo **120**
Roseland	Midtown West **36**
Roxy	Chelsea **59**
Ruby Fruit Bar & Grill	Greenwich Village **84**
Russian Vodka Room	Midtown West **36**
S.O.B's	SoHo **121**
Salon bOb	Lower East Side **133**
Sapphire	Lower East Side **134**
Savoy Lounge	Midtown West **36**
Scharmann's	SoHo **121**
Shark Bar	Upper West Side **15**
Shine	SoHo **121**
Smalls	Greenwich Village **84**
SoHo Grand Bar (SoHo Grand)	SoHo **122**
SoHo Kitchen & Bar	SoHo **122**
Splash	Chelsea **60**
Spy Bar	SoHo **122**
Standard	East Village **106**
Supper Club	Midtown West **37**
Sweet Basil	Greenwich Village **85**
Swing 46	Midtown West **37**
Tar Bar	Upper East Side **24**
Tatou	Midtown East **47**
Temple Bar	East Village **107**
Tenth Street Lounge	East Village **107**
Terra Blues	Greenwich Village **85**
Top of the Tower	Midtown East **47**
Torch	Lower East Side **134**
Tortilla Flats	Greenwich Village **85**
Townhouse	Midtown East **47**
Tramps	Chelsea **60**
Triad (Darkstar Lounge)	Upper West Side **16**

Tribeca Grill	TriBeCa **143**
Trilogy Bar & Grill	Upper East Side **24**
Typhoon Brewery	Midtown East **48**
Union Bar	Gramercy **70**
Vain	East Village **107**
Velvet Rest. & Lounge	SoHo **123**
Venue	Upper West Side **16**
Veruka	SoHo **123**
Village Vanguard	Greenwich Village **86**
Vintage	Midtown West **37**
Vinyl	TriBeCa **143**
Void	SoHo **123**
Von	East Village **108**
Wall Street Kitchen & Bar	TriBeCa **143**
Waterloo	Greenwich Village **86**
Wax Bar	SoHo **124**
The Web	Midtown East **48**
Webster Hall	East Village **108**
Wetlands	TriBeCa **144**
Whiskey Bar (Paramount Hotel)	Midtown West **38**
Whiskey Park (Trump Parc Hotel)	Midtown West **38**
Yaffa's	TriBeCa **144**
Zinc Bar	SoHo **124**

Live Music

Upper West Side

Cleopatra's Needle **13**
Iridium **14**

Prohibition **15**

Upper East Side

Cafe Carlyle **21**
Manny's Car Wash **23**

Merchants NY **23**

Midtown West

Birdland **30**
Copacabana **32**
Don't Tell Mama **32**
Le Bar Bat **35**

Roseland **36**
Savoy Lounge **36**
Supper Club **37**
Swing 46 **37**

Midtown East

5757 **42**
Denim & Diamonds **44**
Monkey Bar **45**

Oak Room **46**
Tatou **47**
Townhouse **47**

Chelsea

Downtime **53**
El Flamingo **54**

Hammerstein Ballroom **56**
Tramps **60**

Gramercy

Blue Water Grill **65**
Jazz Standard **67**

Irving Plaza **67**

Greenwich Village

55 Bar **74**
Bitter End **75**
Blue Note **76**
Bottom Line **76**
Cafe Wha? **77**
Chicago B.L.U.E.S. **77**
The Cooler **78**
Duplex Cabaret **79**

Elbow Room **79**
Gonzalez y Gonzalez **80**
Life **82**
Nells **83**
Smalls **84**
Sweet Basil **85**
Terra Blues **85**
Village Vanguard **86**

East Village

Acme Underground **91**
Astor Rest. & Lounge **91**
Avenue B Social Club **91**
Brownies **94**
C-Note **95**

C.B.G.B. **95**
Fez **98**
Internet Cafe **101**
Izzy Bar **101**
Webster Hall **108**

SoHo

Don Hill's **155**
S.O.B.'s **121**

Velvet Rest. & Lounge **123**
Zinc Bar **124**

Lower East Side

Arlene Grocery **128**
Baby Jupiter **128**
Dharma **129**
Luna Lounge **131**
Max Fish **131**

Meow Mix **132**
Mercury Lounge **132**
Motor City Bar **132**
Rivertown Lounge **133**
Salon bOb **133**

Hotel Bars

Upper West Side

Iridium (Empire Hotel) **14**

Upper East Side

Cafe Carlyle (Carlyle Hotel) **21**

Midtown West

44 (Royalton) **28**
Journey's Lounge-
(Essex House) **34**
Oak Room (Algonquin Hotel) **35**

Whiskey Bar
(Paramount Hotel) **38**
Whiskey Park
(Trump Parc Hotel) **38**

Midtown East

5757 (Four Seasons Hotel) **42**
Bull & Bear (Waldorf-Astoria) **43**
King Cole Bar (St. Regis) **45**

Monkey Bar (Hotel Elysee) **45**
Morgan's (Morgan Hotel) **46**
Oak Room (Plaza Hotel) **46**

Gramercy

Cibar (Inn at Irving Place) **65**

Gramercy Park Hotel **66**

SoHo

SoHo Grand Bar (SoHo Grand) **122**

Cabaret

Midtown West

Kit Kat Klub **34**

Don't Tell Mama **32**

Midtown East

Bill's Gay Nineties **43**
Moscow **46**

Tatou **47**

Greenwich Village

Bar D'O **75**

Duplex Cabaret **79**

East Village

Lucky Cheng's **102**

Cigar Friendly

Upper East Side

Club Macanudo **21**

Lexington Bar & Books **22**

Midtown West

21 Club **28**

Flute **33**

Midtown East

Au Bar **42**
Beekman Bar & Books **43**

Bull & Bear (Waldorf-Astoria) **43**
Oak Room (Plaza Hotel) **46**

Gramercy

Aubette **64**
Blue Water Grill **65**

Cibar (Inn at Irving Place) **65**

Greenwich Village

Hudson Bar & Books **81**

East Village

First **98**

Gemini Lounge **99**

SoHo

Chaos **114**

Magnum **117**

TriBeCa

Bubble Lounge **138**
City Wine & Cigar Co **139**

Knitting Factory **140**

Happy Hour

Upper West Side

Indigo **14**

Upper East Side

American Trash **20**
Brother Jimmy's **21**
Club Macanudo **21**
Hi-Life Rest. & Lounge **22**

Manny's Car Wash **23**
Martell's **23**
Merchants NY **23**
Trilogy Bar & Grill **24**

Midtown West

Bar 54 **29**
Bistro Latino **30**
Cafe Papagallo **31**
Don't Tell Mama **32**
Film Center Cafe **33**

Revolution **35**
Russian Vodka Room **36**
Savoy Lounge **36**
Swing 46 **37**

Midtown East

Denim & Diamonds **44**
Julie's **44**

Townhouse **47**
The Web **48**

Chelsea

Barracuda **52**
Downtime **53**
G Lounge **55**

La Maison de Sade **56**
Splash **60**

Gramercy

Aubette **64**
Kashmir **68**

Lemon **68**
Pete's Tavern **69**

Greenwich Village

Art Bar **74**
Cafe Wha? **77**
Duplex Cabaret **79**

Henrietta Hudson **80**
Monster **82**
Riviera Cafe & Sports Bar **84**

East Village

2A **90**
7B **90**
Ace Bar **90**
Bar None **92**
Bar XVI **92**
Baraza **93**
Barmacy **93**
Beauty Bar **93**
Coney Island High **96**

Continental **97**
Detour **97**
Global 33 **100**
Great Jones Cafe **100**
Internet Cafe **101**
The Library **102**
Nevada Smith's **104**
Nice Guy Eddie's **105**
Pierrot **106**

SoHo

Cafe Noir **113**
Chibi's Sake Bar **114**
Ear Inn **115**
L'Orange Bleue **117**

M & R **117**
NV **119**
The Room **120**

Lower East Side

Arlene Grocery **128**
Barramundi **129**
Dharma **129**
Local 138 **130**
Ludlow Bar **131**

Meow Mix **132**
Orchard Bar **133**
Rivertown Lounge **133**
Salon bOb **133**
Sapphire **134**

TriBeCa

Cafe Remy **138**
Edward Moran Bar & Grill **139**

Knitting Factory **140**
Riverrun Cafe **142**

Comedy

Upper West Side

Triad (Darkstar Lounge) **16**

Midtown West

Caroline's **31**

Greenwich Village

Boston Comedy Club **76**   Comedy Cellar **78**

Lower East Side

Luna Lounge **131**   Baby Jupiter **128**

Gay/Lesbian

Midtown West

La Nueva Escuelita **34**

Midtown East

Julie's **44**   The Web **48**
The Townhouse **47**

Chelsea

Barracuda **52**   Mother **54**
G Lounge **55**   Roxy **59**
East of 8th **54**   Splash **60**

Greenwich Village

Bar D'O **75**   The Monster **82**
Duplex Cabaret **79**   Nowbar **83**
Hell **80**   Ruby Fruit Bar & Grill **84**
Henrietta Hudson **80**

SoHo

Androgyny **112**   Don Hill's **115**